God Knows Me.
Does God Know You?

A CONTEMPORARY DEVOTIONAL

DR. VERONICA JOHNSON

ISBN: 979-8-9900918-0-1
Library of Congress Control Number: 2024908514

Graphic Designer: J. Robinson ~ Digital Media Services, LLC.
Editor: Katherine Adegoke ~ Katherine Editorials

Published by V & J Publishing Company

Printed in the United States of America.

TABLE OF CONTENTS

PART I: THE PRELUDE

PART II: THE INTERLUDE

PART III: THE RECESSIONAL

PART I:
THE PRELUDE

1

JUST SAY YES TO THE LORD

*"The steadfast love of the Lord never ceases to come to an end; they are new every morning; great is your faithfulness." — **Lamentation 3:22-23***

Every day, we are faced with challenges and obstacles that interfere with us seeing the face of God. Then we choose to say yes to everyone who will not say yes to us or even stop to see if they are able to help. It is good to say yes to people, but it is much better to say yes to the Lord. Saying yes to the Lord means you have truly surrendered to His will and to His way. Lamentations 3:22-23 says, "The steadfast love of the Lord never ceases to come to an end; they are new every morning; great is your faithfulness." When we surrender all to the Lord, it is like a freeing spirit; we have nothing at all to worry about. When we give our heart to Jesus, we no longer have to carry the weight of the world on our shoulders. We can soar like an EAGLE because God is now directing and steering the course of our lives. We are no longer the boss but merely an employee of the Lord. Amen.

THINK IT OVER POINTS:

1. Have you totally surrendered to the Lord?
2. Name something that you recently have said yes to the Lord.

Prayer: Lord, help me surrender my life daily to you so that I am able to focus on your word, your will, and your way. Just saying yes to you, Lord, frees me up from the worries of this world. Lord, I thank you for directing my path. I trust you today and forever more. Amen

2

FORGIVENESS

*"But if you do not forgive others of their sin, your
Father will not forgive your sins." —**Matthew 6:15***

True forgiveness is freeing. Matthew 6:15 reads,
"But if you do not forgive others of their sin, your
Father will not forgive your sins." Just sitting at
home thinking about three people that I know have truly
wronged me is uncomfortable. In the past, I said that they
were forgiven, but I truly had not forgiven them. I will not
say their names, but I will say these names: Debra, Patricia,
and Andrea; you are truly forgiven. It does not matter what
is going on or what has happened due to past experiences.
I forgive you, and I forgive myself for holding onto things
that may have cut off my blessings from God. I will not let
death or memories haunt me for the rest of my life. I want
more of God's faith, grace, and mercy. There's nothing that
would separate me from the love of God.

Romans 8:38-39 states, "For I am convinced that neither

death nor life, neither angels nor demons, neither the present nor the future, nor any powers, neither height nor depth nor anything else in all creation will be able to separate us from the love of God that is in Christ Jesus our Lord." People may not love you or treat you how you desire to be loved but remember that is not your problem. Your responsibility is to treat them with the love of Christ despite how you are treated. This step took me years to get to. Although it was my fault. When you know better, you do better. Life is short because a person can be gone within the blink of an eye, but I do not want my days to be shortened because of foolery. True forgiveness is letting go and not holding onto the past. I am so happy since I freed myself from the unforgiveness that I had in my heart.

THINK IT OVER POINTS:

1. Think of a person that you may need to ask for forgiveness. Was the situation so big that you and the person could have resolved the issue much sooner than later?
2. What could you have done differently in the situation?

Prayer: Heavenly Father, thank you for allowing me to see true forgiveness and for allowing me to accept people where they are without judgment. Thank you for allowing me to have one more day to get it right on this side. Amen.

3

TOO LATE

---

*"This is my commandment that ye love one another, even as I have loved you." — **John 15:12***

I should have called, sent a card, or sent a text. I should have stopped by to check on her, but it is too late now. They are gone and out of sight. This is what we say, but it is still heavily on our hearts, and it is too late to do anything about it. John 15:12 says, "This is my commandment that ye love one another, even as I have loved you." A scripture we all know too well, but still, we don't take heed of it. Love is an action word. You must show love to everyone and not base it on how they treat you. It is not necessary in gifts but how you treat them daily. You should not let another day go by without reaching out to someone who has been on your heart and mind.

Philippians 2:4 reads, "Let each of you look out not only for his own interests but also for the interests of others."

Love your family, love your friends, and even love your enemies. Your enemy needs your love the most because they have not experienced true love. Well, that will be in a different devotion. LOL!! Please do not let it be too late. We cannot change the past, but we have now so that we can start today. Start now. Who will you reach out to today? Go and have a great one.

THINK IT OVER POINTS:

1. What is making it difficult for you to reconnect to a family member or a friend?
2. Do you think that God is holding onto things that you did yesterday? Since He is not then, why are you?

Prayer: Let us love one another and be concerned and care for one another while we are here on earth.

4

TELL GOD THANK YOU!

"Oh give thanks unto the Lord, for he is good because his mercy endureth forever." **—Psalm 148: 1**

Everyone has something to thank God for. If you wake up this morning, you ought to say thank you. If you have food on your table, you ought to say thank you, and as far as the season Saints, we would say, "If you are in your right mind, you are to say thank you. My Grandma always said, "If God does not do anything else for me, He has done enough." This all sounds good, so thank you, God, for just being.

Do we really take time to thank the Lord? Do we spend enough time in prayer with the Lord? Do we stop and reflect on just how good our life is and how richly blessed we are? The answer to all of the questions is no. You should be thankful just because of who God is. Psalm 148:1 says, "Oh give thanks unto the Lord, for he is good because his mercy endureth forever." I Chronicles 16: 8

states, "Give praise to the Lord, proclaim his name; make known among the nations what he has done." God has done so much for you, so you should give him glory, honor, and praise. So today, stop what you are doing, stop where you are, and give God glory, honor, and praise, and tell him thank you. Amen.

THINK IT OVER POINTS:

1. Are you truly intentional about giving God the praise, the glory, and the honor?
2. Can you think of something that God has not done for you?

Prayer: Lord, I want to tell you thank you for all that you have done for me and my family. I lifted up my hands to worship you. Everything that I have is because of you and I am thankful that you thought enough of me to bless me. Amen.

5

ALL THINGS

*"And we know that all things work together for good to them that love God, to them who are called according to His purpose." — **Romans 8:28***

I mean all things work together for the good of those who love him. Has there ever been a time when things didn't go your way? Everywhere you turned, things weren't working out, or there seemed to be a roadblock? Well, my friend, I need to let you know something. Romans 8:28 says, "And we know that all things work together for good to them that love God, to them who are called according to His purpose." Yes, I have had a time in my life when my husband and I were trying to buy a house, and all three deals fell through. I was angry at myself, God, and the world. We were homeless, living from motel to motel, because we were banking on at least one of the houses to come through, but they did not. My husband had had enough. He told me to get us out of this dump.

When I tell you all things work together I do mean all things. God gave us a place to live temporarily until we were ready for our new home. A good friend of mine didn't have a way home from church because she had surgery, so I had to drive her home. God allowed me to drop her off at home, and God took me to the next subdivision where I would find my new home. As I am writing this, tears are falling down my face. I now realized that all the three deals on the other houses fell through because they were in school districts that were not ideal for my family. I can rejoice in knowing that it worked out for my good. To me, it seems like my journey may be different from most. My blessings sometimes come in threes. When a door closes, God lets me know bigger and better things are on the way. So remember, when I say all things work together, I mean all. All Things.

THINK IT OVER POINTS:

Can you think of a time that you thought God had forgotten about you and your situation, but after God finished, you were in a much better shape than before?

Prayer: Lord, thank you for blessing me to understand and appreciate your plan for my life. I am thankful for the closed doors because you are designing my path, which allows me to receive bigger and better blessings. I recognize that the Holy Trinity: God the Father, God the Son, and the Holy Spirit, knows what is best for my life, and I will wait patiently for my blessing. I know that I'm a few steps ahead of my celebratory celebration. Amen.

6

WHAT'S NEXT?

"Who, then, are those who fear the LORD? He will instruct them in the ways they should choose."

—Psalm 25:12

ife has many twists and turns, and you may find yourself saying what's next? Well, don't get frustrated and upset when things don't turn out the way you like; instead, choose to choose God and triumph over your situation. As parents, my husband and I had many responsibilities to our children based on their extracurricular activities. Our son played football and basketball, but our daughter played volleyball in middle and high school. She also played club volleyball from 5th through 12th grade. We wrote so many checks that we started questioning whether or not she should play club volleyball. The monthly payments were as high as car notes, and when it was time to go out of town because she was on the traveling team, the bills were astronomical together. Even though it was a rough financial season, in the end, God made a way for us to do it.

Has God made a way out of no way for you? Yes, He has. Psalm 25:12 states, "Who, then, are those who fear the LORD? He will instruct them in the ways they should choose." When we choose God, we let the enemy know that he does not have power over our situation; only God has the ultimate say. James 4:7 reads, "Submit yourselves then, to God resist the devil, and he will flee from you." As long as God is in control what is next should not be your focal point, but keep God as the focal point and He will bring you through. Amen.

THINK IT OVER POINTS:

1. Do you let what's next in your life overpower the goodness of God?
2. How can you get yourself out of the "Whoa is me?" spirit?

Prayer: Lord, help me trust you in difficult situations. Help me to stay focused even when things are going right or wrong. God is in control, and He will catch me before I slip and fall. He will guide my path and footsteps and shine the light on the directions I am traveling. So keep me humble so that I can keep seeing you! Amen.

7

GIRL BYE

"Ask, and it shall be given you, seek, and ye shall forth knock, it shall be opened unto you. 8 For everyone who asks receives, and he who seeks finds, and to him who knocks it will be opened."

— Matthew 7:7-8

People do not want to hear the truth about their situation, but they want to complain to you over and over about the same problems. I believe that I do not have to listen when you already know the answer to your question. Girl bye. Get out of here with the foolishness, the foolish talks, and the foolish nonsense. The word says ask what you want, and it will be given to you. Matthew 7:7-8 states, "Ask, and it shall be given you, seek, and ye shall forth knock, it shall be opened unto you. For everyone who asks receives, and he who seeks finds, and to him who knocks it will be opened."

In this season, we must not stay, talk, dwell, confine, consume, or believe in negative talks and we must not give the devil too much credit or ability to win. We must believe the word of God and love God enough to let him handle the situation. Hey Sista, I love you, but I can't do it. I can no longer go down this road with you. You see, I must say, "Girl, bye to you if you have given the devil more power than God." And another thing is if you are not willing to change the situation or the circumstance, then telling me is not going to help. I can only give you the Word of God, who I trust in every situation. So when I say, Girl bye, it is only in love. You may ruin your day, but please don't try to ruin mine because I am going to give you Girl Bye and have a blessed day. Amen.

THINK IT OVER POINTS:

1. When you have a problem, do you fully trust God to work it out?
2. In what ways should you begin to trust God more?

Prayer: God, help my sisters and brothers gain more faith in you. Help them to trust in you and not to give the devil more power than you. You are their maker and creator, so they must surrender all to you if they desire glory, peace, and happiness. Help them to turn their situation over to you because you are always in control. No matter what the situation looks like. Amen.

8

I DON'T KNOW ABOUT YOU, BUT FOR ME AND MY HOUSE

"But if serving the Lord seems undesirable to you, then choose for yourselves this day whom you will serve, whether the gods your ancestors served beyond the Euphrates, or the gods of the Amorites, in whose land you are living. But as for me and my household, we will serve the Lord." **—Joshua 24:15**

I don't have anything against anyone's religion, but I do know one thing: Joshua 24:15 says, "But if serving the Lord seems undesirable to you, then choose for yourselves this day whom you will serve, whether the gods your ancestors served beyond the Euphrates, or the gods of the Amorites, in whose land you are living. But as for me and my household, we will serve the Lord." Only God wakes me up in the morning. Only God turns tears into joy. Only God turns rain into sunshine. Oh but know this: my God is the maker and the creator of the universe

(Genesis 1:1). So why would I choose to serve someone who did not create me? Good question is what I was thinking, too.

Man alone is uncertain, just like when you go start your car; it may or may not start, but know that God is all God. He does not need booster cables, nor do you need to make an appointment to talk to Him. The phone line is always open to talk to your Heavenly Father. You don't have to leave a message with the secretary so He can get back to you. Only open up your heart, mind, and soul to let things begin to happen for you. God gives you free will and extends to you an invitation to become His disciple. Who wouldn't serve a God like that? Let Christ into your heart so that he can be welcomed into your home. Amen.

Think It Over Points:

1. What examples are you setting for family that demonstrates that you serve the Lord, no matter what?
2. How can model Christ so that your family so that will receive salavation?

Prayer: Heavenly Father, thank you for having dominion over my house. Lord, I will always serve, worship, and adore you. If I had 10,000 tongues, it would not be enough to thank you for watching over us and protecting us. Lord, for anyone who desires to receive the gift of salvation, allow them to do the ABCs to salvation: accept, believe, and confess. Continue to always order my steps and bless me and my family. Thank you, Lord Jesus. Amen.

9

JUST A MOMENT

"Taste and see that the Lord is good; blessed is the one who takes refuge in Him." —Psalm 34:8

Sometimes, you need to take a moment to smell the roses, sip the coffee, taste the fruit, and simply just think about how blessed you are. Psalm 34:8 reads, "Taste and see that the Lord is good; blessed is the one who takes refuge in Him. So, in everything that you do, you should seek the face of God. You should always keep God first. God is so good to you. He loves us when we don't love ourselves. Has not God been good to you? That is why I will bless the Lord at all times, and His praises will continually be in my mouth. (Psalm 34:1).

Then I have to say this in Psalm 34:3: Oh magnify the Lord with me, And let us exalt His name together. When you just take a moment, you realize that God has everything under control. You realize you have never been hungry or had to sleep outdoors, and when you were sick, God healed your body. God even makes your enemies behave. Psalm 37: 1-2 says, "Do not fret because of evildoers, nor be envious of the workers of iniquity. For they shall soon be cut down like the grass and wither as the green herb." When you take a moment, just thank the Lord. Because in that moment, it could be your last breath. Just a moment. Just a moment is all it takes to give honor to God. Amen.

THINK IT OVER POINTS:

1. Can you think of a time that you thought God had forgotten about, but you realized that you forgot to seek him first?
2. Why is it important to take time to just have a moment with God? What are the benefits of it?

Prayer: Lord, let me not forget to take just a moment to think about your goodness and mercy. Just a moment to say thank you. Just a moment to say thank you that I am alive. Let me always just take a moment.

10

IT REALLY TASTES GOOD

" *Study to shew thyself approved unto God, a workman that needeth not to be ashamed, rightly dividing the word of truth.*" **— 2 Timothy 2:15**

Sometimes, I sit and reminisce about one of my favorite restaurants where I have had lunch. Perry's Restaurant has the best pork chops, and I always try to go on Fridays to save a few bucks. The bread is delicious, the pork chops are seasoned to the bone, and the asparagus, "My Oh My," is the best that I have ever tasted. Simply put, the food just tastes good, but I also enjoy tasting my spiritual food. I love to read about Jonah, who was in the belly of the whale for being rebellious. I also enjoyed reading about Ruth because Noami was so appreciative of Ruth's loyalty to her. There are so many tasty stories in the Bible that will increase your spiritual walk by strengthening your faith and your love for God. In order to get the strength, you need to thrive on the Word of God.

Paul said in 2 Timothy 2:15, "Study to shew thyself approved unto God, a workman that needeth not to be ashamed, rightly dividing the word of truth." Just like you enjoy feasting on your favorite meal, then you need to feast on the Bible, which is the Word of God so that you may grow spiritually and be able to defeat attacks that the enemy tries to set for you. Psalms and Proverbs have so many lessons to live by, so you should read them often. If you ever feel down and out, read the Word. If you want to be encouraged, then read the Word. The Word of God satisfies your spiritual soul. Sit down, relax, read, enjoy, and feast upon the Word of God — the Bible, your instruction guide, your road map, and your comfort food for life. Amen.

THINK IT OVER POINTS:

1. What is your favorite go-to scripture when you feel that there is no way out?
2. How does reading the Bible help you overcome difficult battles in your life?

Prayer: Lord, let us not get comfortable with feasting off of physical food when we need more of the spiritual food to live by. Let us stay ready at all times, preparing for battles that can only be fought by the Word of God. Let us not forget to apply the whole armor of God in Ephesians 6 to every aspect of our lives, and let us not forget that we need you in every aspect of our lives. Amen.

THAT'S ALL I NEED

"Rejoice always, pray continually, give thanks in all circumstances, for this is God's will for you in Christ Jesus." —Thessalonians 5:16-18

Have you ever looked out the window and noticed that some folks don't have all the things you have? I know I am blessed with an abundance of things that others lack. But I also realize that with all the stuff that I have, nothing can compare to the greatest gift I have received in my life. Jesus is my greatest gift because He gave all of us the gift of salvation, and that's all I need. With this, He has done enough for me; if he does not do anything else. Material things are nice to have, but they fade into the night when you have a desire to get something as your new toy. I Thessalonians 5:16-18 says, "Rejoice always, pray continually, give thanks in all circumstances, for this is God's will for you in Christ Jesus." While materials are nice to have, they do not compare to the gift of salvation that Jesus gave us all. I suggest that you appreciate what you have because someone somewhere else has much less than you. The richness and blessing that anyone can receive is Jesus Christ. If God is all you need, then He will bless you beyond what you think or imagine. Solomon did not ask for riches, and for that reason, God gave him the riches and glory in I Kings 3:1-15. Instead of worrying about what you do not have, be willing to help someone else who has less than you. Always make God your focal point and not your neighbor having less, you having more, or you coveting someone else's material things or being envious of their family. Do right because you know that God is all that you need.

THINK IT OVER POINTS

If you were to lose all of the material possessions that God has bless you with, what would be one thing that you could thank God for that does not cost money?

How have you been selfish by not praising God?

Prayer: Thank you for being all that I need. Help me to keep focused on my life and continue to help me keep God as the focal point of my life. Amen.

12

I WANT WHAT GOD WANTS FOR ME

"For I know the plans I have for you declares the Lord, plans to prosper you and not to harm you, plans to give you a hope of future." — Jeremiah 29:11

There is a list of things that I can make for myself, but I have come to realize that I want what God wants for me. I desire to have more peace and harmony with my sisters and brothers. I want to be able to give love unconditionally to a person who may not love or care for me. Every day, I want to get up with a purpose in mind: *God, what can I do today to glorify your name? Lord, what can I do to help your people?* God, I want what you want for me today and forever more. Yes, there are certain desires and blessings that I may have in mind for myself, and I can surely ask God what I want, but the main goal for my life is to do the will of my Father and please God. So if things are not right with my family and God wants to change it, then I am ok with it because God has a master plan layout for my life. What I may want for my life is small, but what God has in mind for me is Super Big. Jeremiah 29:11 says, "For I know the plans I have for you declares the Lord, plans to prosper you and not to harm you, plans to give you a hope of future." This lets me know that God will make the best path for my life. Amen.

THINK IT OVER POINTS

1. Why is it so difficult for you to let God create the masterpiece for your life?
2. Has there ever been a time in your life when God had to reconstruct, uproot, or change areas of your life.? How were the changes more beneficial than you thought in the very beginning?

Prayer: Lord, you know what I have asked for, but if your desire is something different, better, or precise, and if it is your will, then I want it. I know you want what's best for me, and your will for my life is for better than I can think or imagine. Thank you for choosing what is best for me and my life.

PRAY FOR YOUR ENEMIES

"But I say to you, love your enemies and pray for those who persecute you." —Matthew 5:44

Yes, I know there are people out there in the Big Wide World who are unkind and unfriendly and may not treat you as a human being. Even if they do not treat you like a friend but as a foe, pray for your enemies. Matthew 5:44 says, "But I say to you, love your enemies and pray for those who persecute you." Are people going to talk about you? Yes. Are people going to lie to or on you? Yes. Are people going to plot against you? Yes. Are people going to scandalize your name? Yes, of course, they are, but we ought to pray for people because God will richly bless you when you do unto others as you would have them do unto you. It is that simple. Love your enemies. Pray for enemies and continue to be obedient to what the Word of God has commanded you to do that is right in God's eyes and not in your own eyes. Amen.

THINK IT OVER POINTS:

1. Roll call: is there someone whom you need to forgive?
2. What has God forgiven you of, but you continue to hold it over your head?

Prayer: Lord, I know sometimes it is hard to love my enemies, but I ask that you teach me how to love them, and I will continue to pray for my enemies each and every day. I am learning in this walk that my enemies have fallen short and sometimes will mistreat me because they do not know how to love themselves. Lord, but there are times that I have fallen short as well. I ask that you richly bless them, and I am asking that no hurt, harm, or danger will come their way. Please forgive them for the things that they do to me because they do not know what they are doing. Thank you for loving me in spite of my shortcomings. Amen.

14

I CAN'T QUIT

---

*"He replied, "Because you have so little faith. Truly I tell you, if you have faith as small as a mustard seed, you say to this mountain, 'Move from here to there,' and it will move. Nothing will be impossible for you." — **Matthew 17:20***

There are times when we may get discouraged, feel defeated, overwhelmed, or just plain fed up, but whatever happens, don't quit. Only God knows the plan for our lives. If God has not given up on us, then we must not give up on ourselves. 2 Timothy 4:7 says, "I have fought the good fight, I have finished the race, I have kept the faith." That's it. That's it all in a nutshell. The focus is on *I have kept the faith*. We have to hang in there just a little while longer and ask God to enable us to finish strong. Life may not be easy, and sometimes it may be rough, but with God on our side. We must hold onto our faith. I am talking about holding onto that mustard-seed faith. Matthew 17:20, "He replied, "Because you have so little faith. Truly I tell you, if you have faith as small as a mustard seed, you say to this mountain, 'Move from here to there,' and it will move. Nothing will be impossible for you." God can handle any situation so that you may get through any obstacle. Amen.

THINK IT OVER POINTS:

Think about any situation you are in that seems impossible. Now, think about just how good God is. Is there anything too hard for God that He cannot help you overcome it?

Prayer: Lord, let me not lose the momentum so that I don't have a want-to-quit attitude. Please allow me to gain that mustard seed type of faith. There may be times when my back may be against the wall, but there is no need to worry. I will give you full control over the situation. Amen.

ONLY IF YOU KNEW

---

*"Trust in the Lord with all of your heart and lean
not to your own understanding. In all thine ways
acknowledge Him and He shall direct your path."*
— Proverbs 3: 5-6

Things often look so easy in the lives of others, but looks are often deceiving. Windows are so funny at times. From the outside and from the eyes of other people, it looks like you have everything together, but on the inside of the house, the windows have a totally different look. Day after day, so many people are faced with rejections. They are told *No* so many times that they do not know what the word Yes sounds like. They struggle, and struggle, and struggle some more, and finally, with God's goodness and mercy, they have a breakthrough. Things are not always what they seem. The end result looks so easy, but It is mind-blowing if you know what the person went through to be where they are. Proverbs 3: 5-6 says, "Trust in the

Lord with all of your heart and lean not to your own understanding. In all thine ways acknowledge Him, and He shall direct your path."

God blesses people who trust and believe in Him and look to Him for everything. Please take your eyes off people and put your eyes on the Lord. When you develop your walk in Christ, God will bless you just as the person that you have been looking into their window. You can experience that same Joy, Peace, and Happiness just by staying faithful, following Jesus' footsteps, and abiding by God's Word. If only you know what your life could be like when following after Jesus Christ. So stop looking into someone else's window; look into your heart, and make sure God resides there. If you have not given your life to Christ, today would be a great day to start. Amen.

THINK IT OVER POINTS:

1. How might you looking in the mirror be a distraction from what God has for you?
2. In what ways can you begin to get out of someone else's window and open your heart to God?

Prayer: Heavenly Father, help me to pattern myself after you. Please do not let me covet someone else's life, but help me to learn, grow, and walk in the Word of God.

Let me not take life for granted, but take each day as an opportunity to serve, honor, and glorify your precious name. Amen.

THE NEXT CHAPTER

"Blessed are all who fear the Lord, who walk in obedience to him. You will eat the fruit of your labor; blessings and prosperity will be yours."
— Psalm 128: 1-2

Life always brings about changes. We get married. Then, have kids, and our spouse and kids become our whole world. Then we become the Victorious Woman when the word says our children will wake up and call us blessed (Proverbs 31:28). As days go by and days lead to months, and months lead to years, and finally, they leave our nest because they are going to school, the military, or just getting out on their own. When we celebrate their success, we also shed tears. We miss the talks, the good times, the corrections, the funny videos that were made. As the tears fall from our cheeks, the phone rings, and one of the kiddos calls to say *hello, just seeing how you are doing, checking to see where Dad is, and calling to say good night.*

As you become an Empty Nester, you move on to something different called the Next Chapter of your life. But no matter what is going on, God is still good. Psalm 128: 1-2 reads, "Blessed are all who fear the LORD, who walk in obedience to him. You will eat the fruit of your labor; blessings and prosperity will be yours." As a parent, you have worked hard to provide for your family, supported the kiddos, and very seldom missed a game or any activity.

Dry your tears and get ready to enjoy the next chapter of your life. Pray more, read more, study more, take walks, go hiking, go shopping, make more whoopies, and then shop again, but it is time for you to celebrate the fruits of your labor that come from being a great parent. Yes, you may worry, but they are adults and may make mistakes because it is time for them to make their own chapter and embrace their own path. You have done your part; now let God do the rest. Breathe, cry once more, and dry your face. On to the next chapter because this time, you will now begin to start taking care of yourself. The End.

THINK IT OVER POINTS:

1. What are some of your greatest fears of letting go of your children? Now, how does that actually work when God is in control over every aspect of their lives?

2. Did you take and follow your own path as a young adult? Then why is it hard for you to let them follow their own path? What are your only options? Simple: pray for them each and every.

Prayer: Thank you, God, for allowing me to be a parent to my children. Help me to let go of my children, so I have placed them in your hands because they are yours. Have your way with them because they are your children? Bless me to make sense of my life. A sense of change is constantly evolving in me and my life. Keep blessing me and guiding my footsteps. I will remain on my knees, seeking your face. Thank you, Lord. Amen.

17

I LOVE ME

*"I will praise thee, for I am fearfully and wonderfully made; marvelous art thy words; and that my soul knoweth right well." — **Psalm 139:14***

Do you know that I love me? I love me so much that I must take care of myself. No one else will love you more than you but God. God loves us unconditionally, which means even if we fall short, God's unfailing love will always conquer all. So, if God loves me, then I must love myself. What does loving yourself mean? It means that you must take care of the one body you have. What does loving yourself look like? It looks like you are spiritually fed and healthy (which means eating the right food with the right amount of nutrition), mentally well, and you take time to do something for yourself.

Psalm 34:8 says, "Oh taste and see that the Lord is good; blessed is the man who takes refuge in him!" So God wants you to love him and wants you to love you. If you love yourself, then you must love every part of you, and everything with you must be in Perfect Harmony. Perfect Harmony is what I call the PH Factor. I call it the PH Factor because your spiritual, mental, physical, and recreational self must be together. Psalm 139:14 says, "I will praise thee, for I am fearfully and wonderfully made; marvelous art thy words; and that my soul knoweth right well." If God made you, and if God fearfully and wonderfully makes you, then God loves you. If God loves you, then you must love your whole PH Factor Self. Amen.

THINK IT OVER POINTS:

1. What can you do today to gain that PH Factor you need to grow?
2. What are the true benefits of being in alignment with God?

Prayer: Lord, I love me, so help me take care of myself, the Whole Me, the PH Factor Me. I want to be a blessing to your kingdom and a blessing to your people, and if I am spiritually, mentally, physically, and the recreational me is not one accord, then I fail you and your people. Help me get myself together so that I can be an effective part of the kingdom work that you have for me. Amen, and thank you, Jesus.

18

I CAN'T SEE OUT OF THE WINDOW

"So God created man in his own image, in the image of God he created them; male and female."
— Genesis 1:27

Sometimes, I am so blinded by my own situations that I can't see out of the window. I get in my feelings and want to pout, moan, and groan about a situation that does not matter. Well, what I know about this is God matters, and I matter to God. How do you know that you matter? It is found in Genesis 1:27, "So God created man in his own image, in the image of God he created them; male and female. God created you for a purpose, not to pout, moan, and groan about frivolous situations that have no meaning in your life.

Psalm 63:3 says it all, "Because thy lovingkindness is better than life, my lips shall praise thee." We should give God glory, honor, and praise just because of who God is. It is important to give praise to your maker and creator. So walk to your window and look out of the window to give God thanks for all of His many blessings. Sing praises of adoration just to say thank you for Your grace, mercy, and goodness. Do a celebratory dance for being able to see with your eyes and smell a new day that you have never seen before. Just remind yourself each and every day just how good God is. AMEN!!

Think It Over Points:

1. As you now look out of the window, how are you able to respond to situations differently?
2. Instead of pouting, moaning, or groaning about a situation, what are things that you can plant in your heart, and what will make it grow?

Prayer: Lord, let me not pout, moan, and groan about things that do not matter. Let me celebrate you for your goodness, grace, and mercy. Psalm 118:24, "This is the day which the Lord hath made; we will rejoice and be glad in it." I am happy for this day, so Lord, I will celebrate you! Amen.

19

LET GO!

"Looking unto Jesus, the author and finisher of our faith, who for the joy that was set before time endured the cross, despising the shame has sat down at the right hand of the throne of God."
—Hebrews 12:2

Yes, devil, let go. You have no control over my life. You might try all you can, but you will not win. Every door you block, God will open another and another and another. Do you know why? Because God is the author and finisher of my faith. Hebrews 12:2, "Looking unto Jesus, the author and finisher of our faith, who for the joy that was set before time endured the cross, despising the shame has sat down at the right hand of the throne of God." Jesus will always direct your path, and He will not let any harm come towards you. Just a large box is used to hold many items, but once you are finished with the box, it is taken out to the trash. That is how the Lord will handle you if you try to mishandle me. He will cut you down and put you out with the trash. So Let's Go because my Father in heaven is more powerful than you. No matter what happens, I will not get discouraged because my Father in heaven tells me to look up. Psalm 121: 1-8 says it all.

Psalm 121:1-8

I will lift up my eyes to the hills-From whence comes my help?
My help comes from the Lord, Who made heaven and earth.
He will not allow your foot to [a]be moved; He who keeps
you will not slumber.
Behold, He who keeps Israel, Shall neither slumber nor sleep.
The Lord is your keeper; The Lord is your shade at your
right hand.
The sun shall not strike you by day, Nor the moon by night.
The Lord shall preserve[d] your going out and your coming in
From this time forth, and even forevermore. Lord shall
[preserve you from all evil; He shall preserve your soul.

Listen devil, I trust God. The word also says touch not thy anointed one and do my prophet no harm. 1 Chronicles 16:22. Rest assured that I am covered and protected by God. In Jesus name, Amen.

THINK IT OVER POINTS:

1. How does God direct your path in a difficult situation?
2. What can you do to continue to focus on the goodness of God?

Prayer: Lord, let me always stay close to you and your word so that the devil will flee from me. I trust you in all situations, even when things are going well or bad. I know this for certain: no matter the situation, you will be there. Let me always give you glory, honor, and praise. Amen.

20

DREAM BIG

"And the Lord answered me, and said: Write the vision and make it plain upon tables: That he that readeth it may run over it." Habakkuk 2:2

Habakkuk 2:2 states, "And the Lord answered me, and said: Write the vision, and make it plain upon tables: that he that readeth it may run over it." To dream big, you must write a vision. If you can dream it and believe it, then you can accomplish it. Our Father in Heaven wants us to be happy. He celebrates us in our victories and He is with us during trials and tribulations. So if you have a plan, make it plain to the Lord. And when you Dream Big, be specific in your asking. Don't say God, I want a new car. Say, God, I want a new car, and the type of car I want is a Nissan Armada. I want a blue one with smooth upholstery. I want air, four wheels, a radio, a navigation system, etc. Lord, I want to pay no more than $550.00 a month for it. Psalm 37:3-4 says, "Trust in the Lord, and do good, dwell in the land and befriend faithfulness." Delight yourself in the Lord, and he will give you the desires of your heart." This is a reassurance that God wants His children to be happy. When I think about the goodness of God, I get so happy because God has done so much for me. Sometimes, I go through trials, and then here comes another trial, but I will continue to celebrate God because He is my all and all, no matter what. I can also take my burdens to the Lord and leave them. Yes, Dream Big and watch God.

THINK IT OVER POINTS:

1. What is holding back from moving forward with God's plans for your life?
2. What is stopping you from Dreaming Big?

Prayer: Thanks for letting me Dream Big and blessing my prayers to come to fruition. No matter what day it is, you are always putting a smile on my face. I don't care about burdens because they are left at the altar. I DREAM BIG because I serve a BIG GOD. Amen.

21

KNOW WHAT YOU WERE DESIGNED TO DO

"Whatever you do, work heartily, as for the Lord and not for men, knowing that from the Lord you will receive the inheritance as your reward. You are serving the Lord Christ." —Colossians 3:23-24

God created everyone for a purpose. Sometimes, people don't know what their purpose is, and they lose sight of what God is calling them to do. For example, I can cook all types of beans. Pinto Beans, Red Beans, White Beans, and Navy Beans are just a few that I can cook. I have also learned that I cook well the things I know how to cook. For example, beans are something I can cook well and easily. When it comes to greens like turnips or mustard, that is something I have never learned to cook to perfection. I will, however, one day master it, but I will not bring that dish to a family outing. I was not designed to make delicious greens at this moment in my life, but I am willing to learn. As a little girl, I seldom worked in the kitchen, and I learned later in my life how to cook. There are things that I am good at and designed to do. God has given me the gift of hospitality, delegating things to others, organizing things, and getting things done. Those are my gifts, and that is what God has designed me to do. So, if the choir is singing, I will not get up to lead a song. I would be out of place and out of order.

Colossians 3:23-24 says, "Whatever you do, work heartily, as for the Lord and not for men, knowing that from the Lord you will receive the inheritance as your reward. You are serving the Lord Christ." We do things well because we want to please God. We also want the blessings and the favor of God. Psalm 90:17 says, "Let the favor of the Lord our God be upon us, and establish the work of our hands upon us; yes, establish the work of our hands!" Make sure whatever you do, you do it for the Lord so that God is well pleased. You may not do or get everything right, but try your best to do it well. On judgment day, you will hear, "His master replied, 'Well done, good and faithful servant! You have been faithful with a few things; I will put you in charge of many things. Come and share your master's happiness!" Those are the words that you are going to want to hear. So remember, Know what you were designed to do because it is all for the Glory and Goodness of God!

THINK IT OVER POINTS:

1. What has God designed for you to do?
2. Are you operating in your gift?

Prayer: God, help me know what I am designed to do. Sometimes as believers, we get sidetracked, and we forget our purpose in life. But let us not forget that whatever we do, He must get the glory, honor, and praise. These blessings we ask in Jesus's Name, Amen.

22

GOD MUST BE FIRST

Jesus replied: "'Love the Lord your God with all your heart and with all your soul and with all your mind." This is the first and greatest commandment.
— Matthew 22

I know sometimes we don't get it right the first time, but in some instances, we are given a second chance. A long time ago, I was in a horrible relationship. This person did not care about me and simply valued me lesser than other people. I took it to heart and became so consumed with the mistreatment that I actually lost myself. I was depressed and suffered from anxiety. Did I love this person more than God? In Matthew 22, Jesus replied, "'Love the Lord your God with all your heart and with all your soul and with all your mind." This is the first and greatest commandment.

I had lost my way. I was so caught up with him and the foolishness that I was almost gone and had moved away from God. God asked me one question, "Who do you love more, me or him?" My answer was so simple, "Lord, I love you and choose you." God said, "Get up out of the closet and let's go work." I had to ask God for forgiveness because I put that person before God. I had made that person a god and gave him power of mind and heart. The bad part about all of this is that the person did not love or care about me. Exodus 34:14 says, "For thou shalt worship no other god; for the Lord, whose name is Jealous, is a jealous God." You can't put anything before God, and that includes family, relationships, work, money, or material things.

After a while, I found moving on to be one of the greatest blessings that could ever happen to me. God and I picked up where I left off, and I got a fresh start with God and a better start with a new relationship. Look at what God has done! God has kept me and has put someone in my life who actually loves me. A true man of God, My Boaz, and my husband.

THINK IT OVER POINTS:

1. Has there ever been a time when you put something or someone before God?
2. If you chose something over God, what did it cost you? What were your regrets?

Prayer: God, help me to always remember to keep you first because you will never leave me nor forsake me. Let me rise up and say thank you every morning. Let me go to bed and say thank you every night. Let me not ever forget how great you have been to me, and thank you for always blessing me and giving me a second chance at life. Amen.

23

IS IT WORTH IT?

"You will keep him in perfect peace, Whose mind is stayed on You Because he trusts in You." **—Isaiah 26:3**

I t is very sad that we are emotional beings. We allow people and situations to get the best of us. We take things personally and waste time in our lives being miserable about nothing. Is it worth it to be mean or mad about something or someone who doesn't even care about the situation at all? Isaiah 26:3 reads, "You will keep him in perfect peace, whose mind is stayed on you because he trusts in you". God wants us to spend our time being happy and keeping our minds focused on Him. If we keep our eyes and hearts on Jesus, then getting upset won't be worth it. Life is not about proving who is right or who is wrong but living each day like it is your last day.

Psalm 118:24 says, "This is the day which the Lord hath made; we will rejoice and be glad in it." Each and every day that you wake up, you ought to shout thank you to God for another day. Thank you, God, for another opportunity to get it right. My family is small, but we have much love for each other. My older brother once told me, "Just because you know the words to a song doesn't mean you have to lead it." I found that so profound because it boils down to not who is right or wrong, but it is about shaking things off and moving forward. God's love for us exceeds any problem, confusion, or disagreement. God is more important than anything. Yes, I said it, anything. We are not worthy of His blessings, but He still blesses us. So today, breathe, sip your coffee, cuddle up with a book, and relax. As you relax, begin to think of all the blessings that He has given you that you did not deserve. And know that getting along with other people is worth it because God is worth it. Amen.

THINK IT OVER POINTS:

1. What do you consider your perfect peace?
2. If God has given you grace, who should you extend grace to?

Prayer: Heavenly Father, thank you for showing me that doing Your Will is worth it. Thanks for the constant reminders that getting along with people is what you expect from all of your children. No matter what type of day I am having, I know that the love you have for me gives me something to smile about. Also, thanks for all of the many blessings I receive daily when I am not worthy of any of your blessings, including grace and mercy. Thank you, God. Amen.

24

YOU NEED TO GO ON A DIET

"Do not conform to the pattern of this world, but be transformed by the renewing of your mind. Then you will be able to test and approve what God's will is— his good, pleasing and perfect will." **—Roman 12:2**

remember when I was a kid, I loved eating at buffet restaurants because there was so much food. Well, not just the fact that there was so much food, but the fact there were so many food choices to choose from the buffet. My eyes would bulge out of my head just because I saw the food, and I wanted to try all of the delicious food. As I ate more food and was past full, I would become sick. The greediness bug definitely got me, and I felt uncomfortable and miserable at the same time. Thinking about it now, I never understood why we would put more food than we could eat on our plates. It was as if we all had spirits of gluttony. That is how life is too, because we tend to take on more responsibilities than God has required us to do.

Colossians 3:23 says, "Whatever you do, work heartily, as for the Lord and not for men." We are so busy that we don't get any rest. We are running here and there, barely getting any sleep, and what does that mean? It means we become ineffective to ourselves and to God. We pile more activities on our plates for ourselves, and then we blame the kids and everyone else. How ironic is it that you blame the kids, but you have committed yourself to signing the kids up for more activities than they can handle? You blame the job, but you have overextended yourself to the job instead of saying No to things that you should not have to do. Our job is to be an Effective Christian.

Roman 12:2 says, "Do not conform to the pattern of this world, but be transformed by the renewing of your mind. Then you will be able to test and approve what God's will is—his good, pleasing and perfect will." Now, all you can do is go on a diet. Remove things off your plate that are overbearing, especially those that take you away from family and, most of all, God. Make a list of things that should be done in a day and other things that are not relevant or important to Kingdom building, and remove them from your plate. Busyness takes us away from God and interferes with us doing God's work. Make God first, take care of your family, and remember to take care of yourself. Push away from things that add more responsibilities than you need to be concerned with and eventually will not give you joy. Do well with things that you are good at so that you will be full and content. Make it a habit to do things that are pleasing to God. Eat well and live well. Amen.

THINK IT OVER POINTS

1. What have you added to your plate that you can easily remove?
2. Can you find a time that you feel you have neglected God? Do you feel that you have you failed to hear the voice of God?
3. What are the first steps to reconciliation?

Prayer: God help me to learn when I am full. Help me to learn when to say that I have enough on my plate. Keep me content and grounded with your word and covered with your blessings. Let me take an important responsibility to share your word and gift of salvation with your people. Amen.

25

OLD WOUNDS

"Let all bitterness, wrath, anger, clamor, and evil speaking be put away from you, with all malice."
—Ephesians 4:31

Unforgiveness is like an old wound that can't heal. You try to move on, and something happens and makes the scab come off, then the healing process has to start all over again. But old wounds don't and shouldn't have that much power over you. If something has been put out of the garbage, then once the garbage man comes, that trash is gone forever. Old wounds should fade away so that you aren't able to see a scar.

Ephesians 4:31 says, " Let all bitterness, wrath, anger, clamor, and evil speaking be put away from you, with all malice." God wants us to Walk in Unity and with Love. Ephesians 4: 1-3 reads, "I, therefore, the prisoner of the Lord, beseech you to walk worthy of the calling with which you were called, with all lowliness and gentleness, with longsuffering, bearing with one another in love, endeavoring to keep the unity of the Spirit in the bond of peace." In all things, you must show love to your enemies, loved ones, and anyone who has wronged you. Sometimes, people mean well, but they don't say it well. So, you must have the gift of forgiveness and the gift of reconciliation.

Matthew 5: 23-24 says, " Therefore if you bring your gift to the altar, and there remember that your brother has something against you, leave your gift there before the altar, and go your way. First be reconciled to your brother, and then come and offer your gift." In order to receive the blessings of God, you have to do your part to get it right with your Sister or Brother. If you have done everything to move on, moved away from old wounds, then you are doing what is right to please God. Do your part! Do your part!! If the person has not done their part after you have made peace, then shake the dust off your feet and move on. There is nothing, and I mean nothing, in the world you have been through that Jesus hasn't experienced. Jesus died on the cross and was innocent. He took on the weight of the world's sin for all of us. Yes, that is love, so move on and trust God. Thank God each day for another opportunity to Get it Right. Amen!

THINK IT OVER POINTS:

1. Make your list quickly. Who is the person that you need to make peace with?
2. Do you believe it is easier to forgive family or friends? What is your response, and why do you feel that way?

Prayer: Lord, let me bury the hatchet once and for all. I have pulled off the over used bandaid on the old wound that has been healed. You suffered the ultimate death on the cross when you died for our sins. Let me not go another day and be miserable when I can have Resounding Joy for all the blessings that you have bestowed. Lord, I thank you, and I love you. Amen.

PART II:
THE INTERLUDE

26

WHY GO BACK?

"God is not a man, that he should lie; neither the son of man, that he should repent: hath he said, and shall he not do it? or hath he spoken, and shall he not make it good?" **—Numbers 23:19**

I know that I am not the only one that does this, but it happens. Everyday before I leave my house, I watch the garage go down, but for some strange reason, I go back to make sure it is down. This makes me so mad because I often waste my time doing this action. There was also a time I would drive back to my house to make sure the iron was unplugged or turned off. If you have ever done any of these things, then you are not by yourself. But isn't that how life is? We fill our day with unnecessary worry because we do not trust ourselves, but an even bigger problem is that we don't trust God. If God said He will do something, then believe Him and take Him for His Word.

Numbers 23:19 says, "God is not a man, that he should lie; neither the son of man, that he should repent: hath he said, and shall he not do it? or hath he spoken, and shall he not make it good?" So, if that is the case, why go back? Why do we go back, doubting, and have feelings of unbelief or uncertainty? One could say it is the fear of the unknown. I beg to differ. I believe we just don't trust God enough to believe that He will come through. Just like we shouldn't go back to check the garage, the iron, or the curling iron, we should not doubt or check to see whether or not God is going to show up for us. We serve the All-Knowing, the Alpha, and Omega. This means God knows all about us and will be with us until the end of time.

Deuteronomy 33:6 says, " Be strong and courageous. Do not be afraid or terrified because of them, for the Lord your God goes with you; he will never leave you nor forsake you." One thing is for sure: we do not have to go back to doubt or unbelief because God will never turn His back on us. Amen.

THINK IT OVER POINT:

1. Do you think it is all right to go back and revisit your past pains?
2. Why are we quick to trust man, but slow to trust God?

Prayer: Heavenly Father, thanks for the constant reminders about how much you care for us. There is no need to doubt you because you have proven yourself over and over again. Help me with my unbelief. I know that man can't be trusted, but I can always trust and count on you.

27

DON'T APOLOGIZE
FOR WHO YOU ARE!!

"Whoever is ashamed of me and my words, the Son of Man will be ashamed of them when he comes in his glory and in the glory of the Father and of the holy angels." —Luke 9:26

I am faith-believing, prayer-kneeling, always-trusting, with faith far exceeding mustard seed. I will not apologize for being in love with my Heavenly Father, who has done everything for me. He sent His Son to die on the cross for little old me. Sometimes, I want to get quiet and not share my testimonies of God's goodness for me and my family, but I refuse to keep my mouth shut.

Luke 9:26 says, "Whoever is ashamed of me and my words, the Son of Man will be ashamed of them when he comes in his glory and in the glory of the Father and of the holy angels." So, what do I do? I open my mouth. I want the world to know how much I love the Lord. Listen up. If you have a problem with that, then I will not apologize for who I am and whose I am. I don't have an identity crisis because I have been identified as the Daughter of the King. God made me with a purpose in mind. I am definitely not an accident; as God's child, I was created to be a blessing to others. Psalm 139:4 says, "I praise you because I am fearfully and wonderfully made; your works are wonderful, I know that full well." So, I will not apologize for being a living and loving vessel for God. God has plans for me. I will worship Him and give Him thanks always. Amen.

THINK IT OVER POINTS:

1. Why is it important to be who you are in Christ?
2. What separates you from other people? How are you different?

Prayer: Thank you for giving me love, life, and purpose. I won't apologize for being a living and working vessel for you. I know that you have plans for my life, and as long as I keep you first, you will continue to guide and direct me on the right path. Amen, Amen, and Amen!!!

28

PRESS PLAY

"Nehemiah said, "Go and enjoy choice food and sweet drinks, and send some to those who have nothing prepared. This day is holy to our Lord. Do not grieve, for the joy of the Lord is your strength."
— Nehemiah 8:10

I remember having a cassette player as a child. One of the buttons functions as play and the other functions as pause. Sometimes in life, we allow situations and circumstances to determine where we are on the cassette player. Nehemiah 8:10 reads, "Nehemiah said, "Go and enjoy choice food and sweet drinks, and send some to those who have nothing prepared. This day is holy to our Lord. Do not grieve, for the joy of the Lord is your strength." Sometimes, we have it on pause for too long. Pause is when we are stuck, confused, upset, and defeated. James 4:8, "Come near to God and he will come near to you. Wash your hands, you sinners, and purify your hearts, you double-minded." But I dare you to press play. When you press play, it shows that God has taken over your life, and you have yielded your life to Him.

James 4:7 reads, "Submit yourselves therefore to God. Resist the devil, and he will flee from you." You now have allowed God to take control. Look at God! Oh, how I love Love JESUS! Amen!! Philippians 4:8 reads, 'Finally, brothers and sisters, whatever is true, whatever is noble, whatever is right, whatever is pure, whatever is lovely, whatever is admirable—if anything is excellent or praiseworthy—think about such things." As you are speaking to your situation, the Holy Spirit is guiding you with the right words not with feelings. Pause means something is preventing you from showing and living your best life in Christ, but when you press play. Hallelujah! Hallelujah!! There is a change that comes over you and inside of YOU! Press play and ditch the pause button in your life.

Think It Over Points:

1. What obstacles have you allowed to put a pause in your life?
2. What items in your life can you begin to focus on so that you can press play in your life?

Prayer: God, thank you for blessing me to press play and remove pause from my life. I want my life to exhibit the characteristics of Christ and not show signs of being upset, confused, or defeated. I trust in you so that I know that pressing play shows that you are the reason that I am who I am in Christ. No longer will I let my problems or situation keep me defeated to a pause, but I will move around and allow you to guide all of my footsteps. Thank you, JESUS and AMEN!!

29

HAVE YOU BETRAYED JESUS?

*"For all have sinned and fall short of the Glory of God." — **Romans 3:28***

think about Jesus being nailed to the cross for my sins, and I realize my actions caused Him pain and harm. I think to myself, have I betrayed Jesus? I realized I am betraying Jesus every time I tell a lie and every time I do things that go against what God has said for me not to do. I also realized I am betraying Jesus whenever I let myself down. I also let my Father in Heaven down. Have you betrayed Jesus?

Romans 3:23 reads, "For all have sinned and fall short of the glory of God." We should continue to exemplify the characteristics of Jesus. You should not try to get away with anything because God sees everything. You should be intentional about doing God's will. John 14:23 says, "If anyone loves Me, he will keep My word, My Father will love him, and We will come to him and make our home with Him. If you want God to dwell within you, then you must work to change your behavior that interferes with how you walk with the Heavenly Father. Your daily goal should be to please Jesus and not betray him.

Matthew 25: 39 states, "And the second is like it: 'Love your neighbor as yourself.'" That verse is so powerful because we must get along with people. We must love people. We must do what is right. That is straight to the point with a boom-bang. Let's not betray Jesus but imitate him by doing things that glorify our Heavenly Father. Amen!

THINK IT OVER POINTS:

1. Can you think of ways that you may have betrayed Jesus?
2. How can you develop ways in your daily walk to become more intimate with Jesus?

Prayer: Heavenly Father, help us not to betray Jesus, but help us to imitate Him. Teach us how to love our neighbor as ourselves, and let us continually read and study the Word of God and live Godly. If we somehow fall short, put Godly people around us to show us our short comings. Let us always remember to Glorify your precious name. In Jesus' name, we pray. Amen!!!

30

PUSH THE RESET BUTTON

*"This poor man cried, and the Lord heard him and saved him out of all his troubles." — **Psalm 34:6***

There are days when you get up and go to work, and the day just does not turn out right. It could be something you did or something someone has said to you, but you need to push the reset button. Psalm 34:6 reads, " This poor man cried, and the Lord heard him and saved him out of all his troubles." There are going to be times when you need someone to save you and allow you to start over. God is forgiving and loving and will not keep a list of your misfortunes to use against you. He will dust you off, stand you back up, and tell you to try again.

You may have to reset your mind. Phillippians 2:5, "Let this mind be in you, which was also in Christ Jesus." You may have reset your heart. Psalm 51:10 reads, "Create in me a clean heart, O God; and renew a right spirit within me." You may have reset your walk. Psalm 1:1-2 reads, "

Blessed is the man that walketh not in the counsel of the ungodly, nor standeth in the way of sinners, nor sitteth in the seat of the scornful. But his delight is in the law of the Lord; and in his law doth he meditate day and night." As you push the reset button, prepare for life to be forever changed by God. A new day will give you a new way to do things and a second chance to get it right with God. Amen.

THINK IT OVER POINTS:

1. Why is it so hard to push the reset button?
2. What can pushing the reset button do for you in your life?

Prayer: Lord, thank you for today. I asked that you allow me to have and push the reset button in my life every day. I will not have to hold grudges because I will take the opportunity to forgive, love, and cherish God's people. Thank you for my reset, Lord. Amen!

31

MY PLEASURE

*"Serve the Lord with gladness: come before his presence with singing." – **Psalm 100:2***

Have you ever noticed when you go to Chick-fil-A restaurant, the attendant says, "My pleasure" at the conclusion of every single order, every single time, no matter the requests? Should we, as believers, have the same attitude about God? Lord, my life is not perfect, but it is my pleasure to serve you with everything that I have.

Psalm 100:2 says, "Serve the Lord with gladness: come before his presence with singing." So, all of my bills may not be paid, but I can say my pleasure, Lord. My pleasure to serve you with gladness because although I don't have everything that I want, you have provided me with everything that I need. Philippians 4:19 reads, "But my God shall supply all your needs according to his riches in glory by Christ Jesus." Lord, my health is not the best, but

I am able to wave my hands, walk from wherever I need to go and speak the words of thanksgiving. My pleasure, Lord, is to serve you no matter what's going on in my life because you are always with me.

Deuteronomy 13:8 reads, "It is the Lord who goes before you. He will be with you; he will not leave you or forsake you. Do not fear or be dismayed." Lord, I will not sweat the small stuff, but I will continue to give you thanks and praise in all situations. I will continue to thank you, even if my children fall off track and take a different path that I would not like. I will still say, Lord, it is my pleasure to serve you. It is my pleasure to say thank you because my children are in the palm of your hands, so I am able to sleep at night. Even though my marriage may not be perfect, It is my pleasure, Lord, to serve you and say thank you for my spouse. My job may not be what I want it to be, but My pleasure. Lord, I may be in between, but Lord, it is my pleasure to serve you in spite of my condition. Your Son Jesus served you without ever complaining about anything, so Lord, help me to be more Like your Son, Jesus. Lord, you are my maker and creator, so I thank you for everything that you do, everything that you have done, and everything that you will do. It is my pleasure, Lord, to be able to serve you with a song on my lips and praise in my heart. Amen.

THINK IT OVER POINTS:

1. In what ways can you show gladness even if this is a difficult season in your life?
2. What is your greatest pleasure in serving God?

Prayer: God, help me be more like your Son Jesus and less like me. Help me to say, "My Pleasure Lord," daily. Help me to serve you in any situation and circumstance because you will always be with me. Thank you, God, for being God all by yourself. My pleasure, Lord, Amen.

32

THERE ARE NO UGLY PEOPLE

"Know that the LORD, He is God; It is He who has made us, and not we ourselves; We are His people and the sheep of His pasture." —Psalm 100:3

God is our maker and creator, so there are no ugly people in the world. God created each and every one of us. He did so in His own image. Think about twins for just a moment. Although twins may look identical, they still have some distinctive features. Psalm 100:3 states, "Know that the LORD, He is God; It is He who has made us, and not we ourselves; We are His people and the sheep of His pasture."

God made us but gave us free will to make decisions about how we are to act. Now, do people have UGLY ways? Yes! They can choose to do whatever makes them feel happy. Regardless of whether they have ugly ways or not, it is up to you to treat them with love. 1 John 4: 7-8 reads, "Dear friends, let us love one another, for love comes from

God. Everyone who loves has been born of God and knows God. Whoever does not love does not know God, because God is love." Since God is love, we must show love to people who have UGLY ways. Please do a self-check to ensure you are not being UGLY to others because we are ALL God's children.

Think It Over Points:

1. It is easy to love someone who loves you back. How can you choose to show love instead of choosing to display ugliness to someone who is ugly to you?
2. We all have ugly ways at times. What can you chisel away so that you can be in a closer walk with your Heavenly Father?

Prayer: Heavenly Father, help us do a daily self-examination of ourselves. Help us, Lord not to have UGLY ways towards your people. Lord, no matter how someone treats us, help us find good in the other person. Even when a person is speaking negatively about us, help us to wear this world as a loose garment. Let us be mindful that each day starts fresh and new for everyone. We must give people a second chance each and every day. Amen.

33

IN THE AUDIENCE

"However, as it is written: "What no eye has seen, what no ear has heard and what no human mind has conceived"– the things God has prepared for those who love him." –1 Corinthians 2:9

Have you ever waited in line to see a show or an event, and after you got there, the show was not all that? That is how it is sometimes with life. Things don't always go as planned. You are just waiting in the audience for your turn. The script you thought about in your heart and mind did not go as planned. When those times occur, you need to practice sitting in the audience and letting God take center stage of your life. 1 Corinthians 2:9 states, "However, as it is written: 'What no eye has seen, what no ear has heard and what no human mind has conceived'– the things God has prepared for those who love him."

God knows what is best for you. If you are sitting in the audience, you are allowing the Lord to guide your path. He is the center stage; He will give you a detailed program that will orchestrate every being of your life. Psalm 37:23 says, "The steps of a *good* man are ordered by the Lord, And He delights in his way." There will be no need to worry. It doesn't matter what comes next or whether you have a leading role. When your time comes, God will move you to the center stage. You will be the main attraction. The tickets will be sold out. The audience will have their eyes on you because you have kept your eyes on God.

THINK IT OVER POINTS:

1. What is keeping you from having God be the center stage of your life?
2. Why is it difficult for you to yield to God in the first place?

Prayer: God, thank you for being center stage in my life. Thank you for keeping me when I could not keep myself. I know that it is alright to sit in the audience because you will make room for my entrance. You will be out front when it is time, but I must keep you first, in front, and be covered by your word. Thanks for making things unimportant to others and making them important to me. Amen!

34

DO WE SERVE A GET-BY GOD?

"But my God shall supply all your needs according to his riches in glory by Christ Jesus." —**Philippians 4:19**

D o you ever take the time to just think about how good God is? Do you take a second to reflect on the fact that no matter how hard it is, God is with you? God does not do the bare minimum because God supplies all our needs and then some. Philippians 4:19 states, "But my God shall supply all your needs according to his riches in glory by Christ Jesus." So no, we do not serve a get-by God. We serve a God who wants us to have the best. We serve a God who wants to give us overflow, but we can't have the best if we lack faith in what He can and will do. Your bank account may be empty, but He still will come through to pay your bills and put food on your table. So stop complaining about what you do not have and thank God for what you do have and what's coming on the way. He is not a get-by God just because you settle for what you think is the best for you when God has more for you.

Just because you have thrown in the towel, God has not given up on you. God is waiting for you to pick up the towel and say, Lord, what is next? God is not a get-by God because when He hears your cry, He listens, and He responds. It is up to you to make up your mind and say, God, I need you. God, I trust you. God, I believe what you can do. God, I know what you can do. Lord, if you have done it before, you will do it again. Allow God to take control of your life, and stop letting doubt control you. The situation may very well not be what you like, but God will never fail. Ride the waves whether you go up and down or even fall off, but your God is more than enough to see you through. We serve a good God, not a get-by God! Amen.

Think It Over Points:

1. Why do so many people classify God by thinking He is limited when He is unlimited in everything that he does for His people?
2. Have you placed God in a box, making Him limited in what He can do?

Prayer: Father, thank you for loving me. Thank you for NOT being a Get By God! Thank you for being omnipresent. Thank you for being omnipotent. Thank you for being omniscient. Lord, let me NOT put limits on you because I know you know what's best for me. Lord, help me speak those things that are NOT as though they were. Help me not to speak less for my life but speak More for my life. Let me understand you shall supply All my needs, and I mean All my needs. Amen.

35

TODAY, I AM ATTENDING A FUNERAL

" Bear with each other and forgive one another if any of you has a grievance against someone. Forgive as the Lord forgave you." **—Colossians 3:13**

I am attending a funeral today, Lord. I am burying things that are not of you. Yes, Lord, I am attending a funeral, and first, I am burying unforgiveness. Colossians 3:13 says, "Bear with each other and forgive one another if any of you has a grievance against someone. Forgive as the Lord forgave you." I am forgiving myself for continuing to not to let things go, not being able to say it is in the past, and it remains in the past. 1 John 1:9, "If we confess our sins, he is faithful and just and will forgive us our sins and purify us from all unrighteousness."

Lord, I am attending a funeral today, and I am burying my unhappiness. Lord, you have given me joy. The word says in Nehemiah 8:10, "The joy of the Lord is my strength." I am at my happiest when I have joy. I cannot look at the bad things, problems, or situations, but I can think of these things. Philippians 4:8 says, "Finally, brethren, whatsoever things are true, whatsoever things are honest, whatsoever things are just, whatsoever things are pure, whatsoever things are lovely, whatsoever things are of good report; if there be any virtue, and if there be any praise, think on these things" Yes, Lord I am attending a funeral, and I am burying feelings of being unloved. John 3:16, "For God so loved the world, that he gave his only begotten Son, that whosoever believeth in him should not perish, but have everlasting life." I know that God loves me. 1 John 4:8, "Whoever does not love does not know God, because God is love." God loves me unconditionally. He is my maker and creator. He designed me with a purpose in mind. God, as I lay to rest unforgiveness, unhappiness, and being unloved, this also lays to rest fear, doubt, and mistrust. As these things are being buried, I am able to stand up with joy, stand up with happiness, and stand up with the Father, Son, and the Holy Ghost! God, thank you for being with me at the funeral because you are giving life to my dead situation. Father, I love you, and thank you.

THINK IT OVER POINTS:

1. Why do we allow unforgiveness and thoughts of being unloved to stop us from being the children of God that we are?

2.   Have you forgiven yourself for past mistakes? Have you forgiven others?

Prayer: Thank you for loving me. Thank you for helping me to bury things that are not of you, and that should not be a part of me. As I bury these things that are draining in my life, I ask that you pour more favor and love back into me. Thank you for being God and God alone because God is LOVE. Amen!!

36

I AM GIVING BIRTH TODAY

"Jesus looked at them and said, 'With man this is impossible, but not with God; all things are possible with God.'" **—Mark 10:27**

I am giving birth today to unlimited possibilities. Mark 10:27 says, "Jesus looked at them and said, 'With man this is impossible, but not with God; all things are possible with God.'" I have hopes, dreams, and ambitions. Many people said that it could not be done and that I could not do it, but I can and I will with God. Yes, as I travel to the hospital of faith and prepare for the birth of unlimited possibilities, I will bear down to push out grace, love, mercy, and many more opportunities. I tune out the contractions of life that say the pain is not worth it; the pain may last too long, but as I give my last push, I smile and see new and unlimited possibilities for my life. 2 Corinthians 9:8 reads, "And God is able to bless you abundantly, so that in all things at all times, having all that you need, you will abound in every good work." I am thankful for God blessing me with new and unlimited possibilities. My faith is strong, and I TRUST GOD! Amen!

Think It Over Points:

1. Name a time when you thought that a situation could not be changed, but God turned it around.
2. What can you do to change the thought processes that you have had over time in your heart and mind?

Prayer: Thank you for blessing me with new and unlimited possibilities every day. Nothing is too hard for you, so I trust you. You will always lead me and God on the right path. Amen!

37

WHO ARE YOU A REPLICA OF?

"For in him all things were created: things in heaven and on earth, visible and invisible, whether thrones or powers or rulers or authorities; all things have been created through him and for him."
—Colossians 1:16

I was sitting in my living room just thinking about how awesome God is and how I love the Lord. First, I am in awe because God made me, designed me, and had a purpose in mind for me. Colossians 1:16 reads, "For in him all things were created: things in heaven and on earth, visible and invisible, whether thrones or powers or rulers or authorities; all things have been created through him and for him." This means I am special like no other, and God created me for a reason. Jeremiah 29:11 reads, "For I know the plans I have for you, declares the LORD, plans to prosper you and not to harm you, plans to give you hope and a future."

God has plans for me, and the plans will be wonderful, and you know why because they were designed for me. I can only be me, and you can only be you. The ONLY replication that I need is to resemble Christ. 1 Peter 2:21 states, "To this you were called, because Christ suffered for you, leaving you an example, that you should follow in his steps." I will not try to be like my sister, brother, neighbor, friend, and even parents, but I will resemble and represent Christ so that God in heaven will be glorified. I will forever look like and Stunt like my Father, God in Heaven. Amen!!

Think It Over Points:

1. In this walk of life, why is it important to resemble Christ and not the people of the world?
2. Why is it so important to embrace who God called you to be?

Prayer: Lord, help me embrace the person you created me to be. Help me to be a replica of you and not try to be an imitation of anyone else. Let me follow after the life of Christ by displaying the love of Christ to all of your children. Amen.

38

LET'S SIP SOME TEA

"Taste and see that the Lord is good; blessed is the one who takes refuge in him." —Psalm 34:8

How often do we complain about life and accept things that are not going well? How often do we find that we are truly the REAL problem when things are going wrong? This happens all the time, yet we need to think about the goodness of God. Psalm 34:8 reads, "Taste and see that the Lord is good; blessed is the one who takes refuge in him." Do you know no matter what is going on, you can find refuge in the Lord, peace in the Lord, comfort in the Lord, and love in the Lord? Philippians 4:19 reads, " But my God shall supply all your needs according to his riches in glory by Christ Jesus." God will always take care of you no matter what the circumstances are, so you always find joy in Jesus.

So let's sip some TEA and toast to everything that is good. He woke you up this morning; sip some TEA. He gives you health and strength; sip some TEA. He protects you from hurt, harm, and danger; sip some TEA. 1 Peter 5: 6-7 states, "Humble yourselves, therefore, under God's mighty hand, that he may lift you up in due time. Cast all your anxiety on him because he cares for you." God cares for His children, so let's celebrate the goodness of God and stop complaining about things that do not matter. As Phillippians 4:4 says, "Rejoice in the Lord always: and again I say, Rejoice," this is an example of how and why we should have joy in our hearts for Jesus. Everything may not be great, but everything with God is surely Umm Umm good.

Think It Over Points:

1. How can you find good when disasters may be all around you?
2. Name something that you have complained about this week, but then realize that you were more blessed than your co-worker..

Prayer: Lord, just thank you for being so umm umm good. Things may not be perfect, but your perfection will certainly be what you have for my life. Father God, let me sip some TEA so that I am able to Toast to -Everything that is Good– About God.

39

FINDING THEIR WAY

"Train up a child in the way he should go, And when he is old, he will not depart from it." **—Proverbs 22:6**

I love being a parent, but I have learned over time that children must find their own way. As a parent, It is important that you teach your child how to develop a relationship with our Heavenly Father. Proverbs 22:6 says, "Train up a child in the way he should go, and when he is old, he will not depart from it." Being able to support them is one thing, but trying to control every aspect of their lives to protect them from disappointment, breakdowns, breakups, or any situation is not your job; it is the Lord's.

Take several steps back and allow the Lord to lead them. Give Him full control over their life, and He will guide their path. Proverbs 3: 5-6 reads, "Trust in the Lord with all your heart and lean not on your own understanding; in all your ways submit to him and he will make your paths straight." If you can trust in the Lord for your life, what about your children? I must admit that I am a control freak, so being able to give my children to the Lord was hard, but I soon realized that if God has me, He also has my children. Then, I accepted the fact that letting go and allowing them to find their own path would prepare each one of them for the future. Finding their way would allow God to direct their distinct path for them. Loving them is letting go and giving God the reigns to their lives. Pray, Talk to God, and Watch Him Work! Amen!

THINK IT OVER POINTS:

1. Why do you think it is so hard to release control over your children?
2. Do you believe that you were the perfect child? You probably were not, so why do you expect your child to be a perfect little angel?

Prayer: Lord, help us to allow our children to grow up as children in Christ. As they become young adults, allow us to release control to you and trust the process. God, you are head over our lives, and we know you are going to be head over their lives as well. If our children happen to fall short, help us realize that we all have fallen short before. As we have fallen short, we were able to recover and bounce right back. As you have given mercy to your children, help us to give mercy to our children. Lord, please keep our children covered. Amen.

GOD VALIDATES ME

*"Open up before G*OD*, keep nothing back; he'll do whatever needs to be done. He'll validate your life in the clear light of day and stamp you with approval at high noon." —Psalm 37: 5-6*

As I grew as a child, my mother and I were not very close because she chose other people over me. This was so hard and difficult because I always wanted to hear that my mother was proud of me and loved me. Her words towards me were painful, and they cut like a knife. I would hear, "You will never be anything good in life. You are worthless. I wished you were not born." This sounds cruel and harsh, but it is so easy to let words dictate and channel your fuel to just quit and not move forward. Those painful words motivated me to be who I am today. Psalm 37: 5-6 reads, "Open up before GOD, keep nothing back; he'll do whatever needs to be done: He'll validate your life in the clear light of day and stamp you with approval at high noon."

As time moved on, I realized I did not need people to validate my worth. God validates me in every aspect of my life. Man changes like the weather. It can be cold now, and in the next five minutes, it will rain. Again, man changes often, and that is how we are built, but God remains the same in all seasons of our lives. Later on in my life, I found out that my Grandmother treated my mom differently from her siblings. There you go! A generational curse was soon cut off and stopped with me! Jeremiah 1: 5 reads, "Before I formed thee in the belly I knew thee; and before thou camest forth out of the womb I sanctified thee, and I ordained thee a prophet unto the nations." God knew me before my parents met, and He knew I was destined for excellence right from the start.

God loved me so much that His son, Jesus, died on the cross for me and got up with all power. This means God validates my worth, my being, my soul, my spirit, and every aspect of me. I am important to God. I am valued and loved by God; He validates me. God has the final say, so he holds the key to every aspect of my being. Would I change anything about my life? No, I would not. Why would I not change my life? Because of the struggle and difficulty that were caused by painful words from the one I was close to, I continued to trust God in every aspect of my life. If

I don't get cards, gifts, flowers, or anything from anyone, it does not matter because God loves me, cares for me, adores me, and guess what else? God validates me each and every day by telling me to rise and shine. Today is a beautiful day because you are in it. Amen.

THINK IT OVER POINTS:

1. Why do people crave validation from others?
2. What happens when a person receives the wrong type of validation from other people? How might other people's validation cause severe damage to a person's life?

Prayer: Father God, help me to be more like you. Help me understand that validation of man is not important as long I know you validate me. I will become stronger and wiser just by staying focused on you. Thank you for creating me and choosing me to be the woman of God that I am without needing validation from others, but only by you.

41

WHAT IS THE SITUATION?

"The Lord is my light and my salvation; whom shall I fear? The Lord is the strength of my life; of whom shall I be afraid?" **—Psalm 27:1**

Have you been in a situation where you felt you would not make it? Then you realize that the situation did not belong to you but to God. Psalm 27:1 reads, "The Lord is my light and my salvation; whom shall I fear? The Lord is the strength of my life; of whom shall I be afraid?" What is it to fear? What is the situation? What are you so worried about? Turning the situation over to God means God has it ALL under control. Taking your hands off the situation and giving God full control is your job and part of your responsibility.

Psalm 24: 8-9 reads, "Who is this King of glory? The Lord is strong and mighty, the Lord is mighty in battle. Lift up your heads, you gates; lift them up, you ancient doors, that the King of glory may come in." Lifting up your hands means you surrender all to Him. What situation? Yes, that situation belongs to God! There is no need to worry because God is better for you than all your insurance coverage. God is better than all the money in the world, which you do not have. The situation may seem bleak and doomed, but the situation is not more powerful than God. Psalm 28:7 reads, "The Lord is my strength and my shield; my heart trusts in him, and he helps me. My heart leaps for joy, and with my song I praise him." Again, what is the situation when you have God?

THINK IT OVER POINTS:

1. Why do you allow your problems or situations to seem more powerful than God?
2. Has there ever been a problem that God cannot solve?

Prayer: Lord, help us stay focused and not be consumed by any situation; help us to be consumed in faith in you. There may be times that I want to throw in the towel, but on those days, it helps to look to the hills where our help comes because our help comes from you. Amen!

42

CATCH THE BALL, BUT DON'T DROP IT

"The end of all things is near. Therefore, be alert and of sober mind so that you may pray." **—1 Peter 4:7**

I have a few friends whose children play baseball and softball. Their children love to swing the bat to hit the ball and score points to run. That may seem easy, but going to the field to give the other team an opportunity to hit the ball for points and score runs may not be fun. You must be able to catch the ball and not drop the ball. In the game of baseball, you will not always catch the ball, so balls are going to hit the ground. Sometimes, we get so busy doing different things that we drop the ball. We must be consistent with our walk with God. 1 Peter 4:7 reads, "The end of all things is near. Therefore be alert and of sober mind so that you may pray".

When we become too busy, we lose sight of God. We can't catch the ball because we are all over the place, but the atmosphere changes when we relax and focus on Him. Ephesians 6:12 reads, "For our struggle is not against flesh and blood, but against the rulers, against the authorities, against the powers of this dark world and against the spiritual forces of evil in the heavenly realms. If the enemy can make you take your eyes off Jesus, then he is winning the battle. Psalm 91: 14-15 states, "Because he loves me," says the Lord, "I will rescue him I will protect him, for he acknowledges my name. He will call on me, and I will answer him; I will be with him in trouble, I will deliver him and honor him." Even if you falter God still has you. I believe that needs to be repeated, "Even if you falter, God still has you."

THINK IT OVER POINTS:

1. If you drop the ball, that may mean that you have too much on your plate. What are you doing right now that you should not be doing?
2. What do you do when you realize that you are not following the assignment God gave you?

Prayer: Lord, thank you for teaching me how to handle situations when I have dropped the ball. As times go on, enable me to learn from my mistakes and recover quickly. Help me, Lord, to keep my eyes stayed on You, Jesus. Amen!

43

TASTE THE CHANGE

*"Therefore, if anyone is in Christ, the new creation
has come: The old has gone, the new is here!"*
—2 Corinthians 5:17

Wow, it takes courage and strength to see a needed change and then act on it. Sometimes change can put a bitter taste on our tongue, but when the change is manifested, it puts a great taste in our mouth. 2 Corinthians 5:17 reads, "Therefore, if anyone is in Christ, the new creation has come: The old has gone, the new is here!" Experiencing something new, being able to find the good in it, and being shocked about what has just happened is exhilarating. This can be so refreshing because when you see an orange, you see the hull of the orange, and it is bitter to bite into it, but I dare you to pull away the hull and get to the inside of the orange. It simply quenches your thirst and sweetens your taste buds.

Right now, you are at the delicious stage of your change, so continue to sit at the table for a minute and sober in the goodness of change. I say, bite in and enjoy! Isaiah 43:19 says it all, "See, I am doing a new thing! Now it springs up; do you not perceive it? I am making a way in the wilderness and streams in the wasteland." When Christ is in your life, it is never the same. You see things vividly and clearly, and guess what? Life just tastes different, better, refreshed, and new. Always stop to smell the rose, and never forget to taste the change in your life.

THINK IT OVER POINTS:

1. Name something in your life that needs a do-over.
2. How can the do-over make your life so much better right now?

Prayer: Lord, help me to always appreciate the beauty of life in itself. Let me always stop to give you glory, honor, and praise because life tastes that much sweeter as long as I am walking and fellowshipping with you. Thank you, Lord! Amen!

44

WHAT ARE YOU DRINKING?

"They gave him vinegar to drink mingled with gall, and when he had tasted thereof, he would not drink." —Matthew 27:34

Have you been to a restaurant, and the waiter asks you what you will be drinking? Some people may prefer water, iced tea, cola, or maybe a glass of wine, but what you should not drink is a glass of pity. People like to drown themselves in negative and disappointing things, or they just prefer to stay stuck in a rut for too long. When Jesus was on the cross and asked for something to drink, He was given water and vinegar. Matthew 27:34 reads, "They gave him vinegar to drink mingled with gall: and when he had tasted thereof, he would not drink." If Jesus did not drink or enjoy that bitter taste that was not of substance, why do we enjoy drinking from the cup of misery, defeat, and doubt?

Ephesians 3:20 reads, " Now to Him who is able to do exceedingly abundantly above all that we ask or think, according to the power that works in us." There is nothing that God cannot do; we must be willing to drink from a different cup. 1 Peter 5: 7 reads, "Casting all your care upon Him, for He cares for you." God wants the very best for His children, so we should not settle for the melancholy: I can't, it's not possible, I am not good enough, do you know where I am from? I don't meet the criteria. The truth of the matter is that you are just right for the new cup. Psalm 23:6 reads, "Surely goodness and mercy shall follow me All the days of my life; And I will dwell in the house of the Lord forever." Surely goodness and mercy let you know that in your new cup, God will never leave you nor forsake you. You can leave your doubts and worries at the altar and follow Jesus, because with the love that He shows you, your cup will runneth over.

THINK IT OVER POINTS:

1. Why is it so easy to drink from a bitter cup instead of something fresh and renewed?
2. What are some ways that you can turn your negative thinking into positive?

Prayer: Lord, thank you for helping us drink out of a new cup that shows us the goodness of God daily. Help us to be more confident in you and not give more confidence to doubts and worries. Lord, help us to tune in to the things of God which matter the most. Amen.

45

MISSED IT BY ONE

"These things I have spoken to you, that in Me you may have peace. In the world, you will have tribulation, but be of good cheer, I have overcome the world." —John 16: 33

I remember taking my teacher's state exam, and I missed it by one point. I took the test over 18 times. I felt defeated and ashamed, and I wanted to have a pity party and wanted everyone to feel sorry for me. It was kind of like a 'Woe is Me' kind of party. What I soon learned is that I may have failed the test, but I had not failed at life. I missed it by one, so what? I fell off one side of the horse and then climbed on the other side of the horse and began the ride of my life. John 16: 33 states, "These things I have spoken to you, that in Me you may have peace. In the world, you will have tribulation, but be of good cheer, I have overcome the world."

No matter what you are going through, there is still comfort in God. 2 Corinthians 1:3 states, "Blessed *be* the God and Father of our Lord Jesus Christ, the Father of mercies and God of all comfort." More than anything, I am an overcomer. 1 John 4:4 reads, " Little children, you are from God and have overcome them, for he who is in you is greater than he who is in the world." No one is perfect, and sometimes you will fail, but it does not mean it is over. If you fail, take time to review and examine what has happened. Ask God what you need to learn from this, and then move forward to see how the situation has made you a better person. Then, always give God gratitude by thanking Him for giving you another opportunity to get it right on the next go-round. Failing is not easy, and failing is not forever, but it enables you to trust God no matter the situation. Missing it by one brings you closer to God by three: the Father, Son, and the Holy Spirit. Amen!

Think It Over Points:

1. Why do we give the enemy too much control over our lives?
2. What is a powerful way that can encourage you to move on in spite of your failures?

Prayer: Lord, thank you for my failures and my mistakes. Teach me not to dwell on them but learn from them. Although things may not happen the way I want them, I know that you desire the best and perfect will for my life. I thank you for blessing me and helping me grow closer to you in every aspect of my life. Being a better me helps me to grow stronger in you and in the faith of Christ. I love you now and forever more. Amen!

46

NOT BEING IN A STORM

"Be strong and courageous. Do not be afraid or terrified because of them, for the Lord your God goes with you; he will never leave you nor forsake you." **—Deuteronomy 31: 6-8**

I t is no joke that we want to skate through life without any problems or situations that impact us, but things do happen. Being in the storm is not the problem, but how you handle yourself while going through the storm. Deuteronomy 31: 6-8 reads, "Be strong and courageous. Do not be afraid or terrified because of them, for the Lord your God goes with you; he will never leave you nor forsake you." This scripture encourages me because no matter how big the storm, God will not leave you nor forsake you. He is right there the entire time, helping you, encouraging, covering, and protecting you. Yes, it may not be easy being in a storm, but it is so much better when my Heavenly Father is providing the raincoat (Holy Spirit), umbrella (the Word of God), and rain boots (this lets us know that Jesus is walking with us).

While in the storm, stay on your bent knees. Keep looking at the hills which cometh your help because your help comes from the Lord (Psalm 121: 1-2). Remember you must always fight the good fight of faith (1 Timothy 6:12). Isaiah 40:29-33 reads, "He gives strength to the weary and increases the power of the weak. Even youths grow tired and weary, and young men stumble and fall, but those who hope in the Lord will renew their strength. They will soar on wings like eagles; they will run and not grow weary; they will walk and not faint." You may be on the edge of your seat waiting and wanting to quit, but I dare you to call and cry out to God because He will move on your behalf. Jeremiah 29:11 gives you more hope to live by, and it reads, "For I know the plans I have for you," declares the LORD, "plans to prosper you and not to harm you, plans to give you hope and a future." This lets us know that we are going to come out of the situation better than we went in. Continue to give God the glory, honor, and praise, and watch God work. Many blessings to you and hammer down while you are going through it because you are not by yourself; your Heavenly Father is with you. Amen!

THINK IT OVER POINTS:

1. Why are storms necessary for growth?
2. Name some lessons that can be learned by going through, in, or coming out of a storm.

Prayer: Heavenly Father, going through the storm may not be pretty or what I like, but help me steer the course and trust and believe in you. I am coming out. I will come out like pure gold. I will come out new. I will come out better. I will come out blessed. Lord, help me to focus on these things in Philippians 4:8, "Finally, brethren, whatsoever things are true, whatsoever things are honest, whatsoever things are just, whatsoever things are pure, whatsoever things are lovely, whatsoever things are of good report; if there be any virtue, and if there be any praise, think on these things." Amen!

47

KNEE BATTLES

"Cast your burden on the Lord, And He shall sustain you; He shall never permit the righteous to be moved." —Psalm 55:22

James 4:10 reads, "Humble yourselves in the presence of the Lord, and He will exalt you." There are things in life that you will not have control of. You don't know why or how, and you can't seem to understand what has just taken place. In those instances, you fight with your hands, you fight with your mouth, but you must get on your knees to fight the situation. Those types of fights are called KNEE Battles! You get on your knees and cry out to the Lord with everything you got.

Psalm 55:22 states, "Cast your burden on the Lord, And He shall sustain you; He shall never permit the righteous to be moved." When you cry out to the Lord, God hears you. You compel God to move on your behalf. Psalm 34:6 reads, "This poor man cried out, and the Lord heard *him,*

And saved him out of all his troubles." 2 Chronicles 14:11 reads, "And Asa cried unto the Lord his God, and said, Lord, it is nothing with thee to help, whether with many, or with them that have no power: help us, O Lord our God; for we rest on thee, and in thy name, we go against this multitude. O Lord, thou art our God; let no man prevail against thee."

God knows how you feel. He knows everything about you and everything about your situation, but you must stay on your knees to empty your heart, clear your mind, and give total control over to the Lord. Knee battles humble you, enables you to surrender the situation and allows you to praise God for whatever outcomes because God knows what is best for you based on your situation. As you are on your knees, thank God in advance for His blessings and thank Him for allowing you an opportunity to be humbled in His presence. As your tears fall, know that God is with you and will never leave your side. Amen!

Think It Over Points:

1. Why are knee battles so important?
2. Has there ever been a knee battle that you were not victorious?

Prayer: Heavenly Father, bless me to be humble and earnestly seek you daily. Thank you for the Knee Battles because it enables me to empty my heart and mind to you. As I fall on my knees, let me also have a prayer of thanksgiving in my heart because you are worthy of all the glory, honor, and praise. Amen!

PART III:
THE RECESSIONAL

48

THIS CAN'T BE ALL

"A wife of noble character who can find? She is worth far more than rubies." **—Proverbs 31:10**

God has so much more for us, so this can't be all. God made women beautiful. We are some beautiful creatures. Everyone on earth is shaped differently and has a different personality. I believe sometimes, as women, we just don't love ourselves enough that we settle for any relationship. We get into relationships that have no value and no worth. Proverbs 31:10 reminds us, "A wife of noble character who can find? She is worth far more than rubies." Rubies are very expensive and worth a large amount in currency. If a woman values herself, then she would not allow someone to disrespect her character because she is valuable. Being in a relationship with someone who does not respect you is not how God wants you to be treated. Remember, this can't be all because God wants more for you because he created you to be more valuable than a ruby. Take time to examine yourself to see how much you are worth to yourself so that you will embrace just how valuable you are to God!

Think it over points:

1. When God has more for us as His children, why do we settle for less?
2. If you are a ruby, then you are precious. Why do you devalue yourself?

Prayer: Heavenly Father, I know this can't be all. Help me to embrace the love you have for me daily. Help me to value myself more and appreciate who you created me to be. I will not take shortcuts in a relationship to ensure that my partner values me the way God values me. Amen.

49

THE REARVIEW MIRROR

"He lifted me out of the slimy pit, out of the mud and mire; he set my feet on a rock and gave me a firm place to stand." —Psalm 40:2

Sometimes, your life can feel like you are in a slump. You have moved forward, but now you are in a rut. The blessing in this is that God has been with you through it all. Look into the rearview mirror of your life and see just how far the Lord has brought you. Psalm 40:2 allows me to thank God daily from whence I came. It says, "He lifted me out of the slimy pit, out of the mud and mire; he set my feet on a rock and gave me a firm place to stand."

Many years ago, I knew my daughter would soon go to high school. God showed me it was time to move. I told my husband it was time to sell the house. He was not happy about it, but he would not argue with God. Our house sold in six days thanks to Ashauna, my wonderful realtor and sister friend. The problem was that all three houses that we had contracts on fell through. We were officially homeless. We were living in hotels, motels, and holiday inns. There were other times that we stayed with family. I cried out to God, and he heard me. Losing the three contracts was simply a blessing and God's divine plan. We got the new house in the neighborhood that we wanted. My daughter graduated from the school where we wanted her to be. As I look in my rearview mirror, I can tell God thank you. As I look to see where God has brought my family, I can tell God thank you. God is so good to me.

Psalm 8: 4-9 says it best:

"What is mankind that you are mindful of them, human beings that you care for them? You have made them a little lower than the angels and crowned them with glory and honor. You made them rulers over the works of your hands; you put everything under their feet: all flocks and herds, and the animals of the wild, the birds in the sky, and the fish in the sea, all that swim the paths of the seas. Lord, our Lord, how majestic is your name on all the earth!"

Think It Over Points:

1. Do you think your plans are greater than what God has for you?
2. Can you think of a time that God said no, and you were blessed with something much better?

Prayer: Heavenly Father, thank you for the life lessons that you have taught me from my rearview mirror. Although things may not have gone the way I would have liked, your plan for my life has always proven to be better. Thank you for the word being a lamp to my feet and a light to my path. You are an awesome God. Amen!

50

TELL THE DEVIL NOT TODAY

"But the Lord is faithful. He will establish you and guard you against the evil one." – 2 Thessalonians 3:3

I am on a mission, so I must be clear that the devil has no power in my life. He tried it on the way to work, and I had to remind him of who my daddy was. He tried in my bank account, but I laughed at him. Money may not be what I have, but my Daddy has it all. I make sure the devil knows that he is not just small but that he is a nonfactor in my life. When I keep my eyes on Jesus, the devil has to flee. 2 Thessalonians 3:3 states, "But the Lord is faithful. He will establish you and guard you against the evil one." The Lord can save you and protect you. It can be found in 2 Timothy 4:17, which reads, "But the Lord stood by me and strengthened me so that through me the message might be fully proclaimed and all the Gentiles might hear it. So I was rescued from the lion's mouth." When you have had enough, and you know God has you covered all over, then you can say to the devil, not today. Amen.

THINK IT OVER POINTS:

1. Why should you tell the devil NO the first thing in the morning?
2. In what ways can you relinquish the devil's powers that he thinks he has?

Prayer: Father God, thank you for allowing me to tell the devil not today. Lord, help me use wisdom in every aspect of my life. Let me not give the devil any more power than he thinks he has. Amen!

51

REASSESS THE PROBLEM

---

*"You hypocrite, first take the plank out of your own eye, and then you will see clearly to remove the speck from your brother's eye." – **Matthew 7:5***

Have you ever met anyone who just seems not to get along with people? It is always the other person's fault. Someone is always trying to get them. In that situation, you must reassess the problem. The problem is probably you. Yes, you are the problem. Matthew 7:5 reads, "You hypocrite, first take the plank out of your own eye, and then you will see clearly to remove the speck from your brother's eye." You are so busy finding fault with others that you can't see your own faults. You must be able to see where you fall short so that you can learn from it and move forward. If you have trouble loving others, then learn to love others. Romans 13:8 reads, "Let no debt remain outstanding, except the continuing debt to love one another, for whoever loves others has fulfilled the law." If you have trouble with forgiveness, then you read Matthew 18: 21-22. It reads, "Then Peter came to Jesus and asked, Lord, how many times shall I forgive my brother or sister who sins against me? Up to seven times? Jesus answered, 'I tell you, not seven times, but seventy-seven times.'" As you reassess the problem, please search yourself to ensure that you treat your neighbor, family, friends, and enemies with the love of Jesus Christ. If you work on this, then God will do the rest.

Think It Over Points:

1. Do you think it might be you when things are going chaotic?
2. If you find out you are the problem, how do you handle it?

Prayer: Heavenly Father, thank you for allowing me another opportunity to get it right. Let me not complain about others, but help me to be grateful for the blessings that come from people. Help me to be determined to follow peace with all men. Amen!

52

FINDING PEACE

"And the peace of God, which transcends all understanding, will guard your hearts and your minds in Christ Jesus." —Phillippians 4:7

Many people work a 9 to 5 job and are probably busy from start to finish. They are constantly on the go. Meetings, lunches, meetings, complaints, going to work in traffic, coming home from work with more traffic, and others can't find a job and yet do not have any peace. Finding peace is one in a million. I pray in the morning and read the Word because that gives me peace and it helps to start my day. Phillippians 4:7 reads, "And the peace of God, which transcends all understanding, will guard your hearts and your minds in Christ Jesus." God gives you perfect peace when you put him first. Bills may not be paid, but you have peace. Children may be wayward, but you have peace.

2 Corinthians 13:11 reads, " Finally, brothers and sisters, rejoice! Strive for full restoration, encourage one another, be of one mind, and live in peace. And the God of love and peace will be with you." The phrase live in peace speaks volumes. You must find peace and have peace no matter what is going on in your life, with your family life, at your job, in your church, with your friends, or even with your spouse. You may not live in the biggest house, you may not drive a fancy car, or you may have millions of dollars in the bank, but the greatest blessing to have is peace so that you can rest at night and sleep in the arms of your Heavenly Father. Amen!

THINK IT OVER POINTS:

1. Why do you believe that so many people do not have peace?
2. Why is peace worth more than all the money in the world?

Prayer: Heavenly Father, help me find my peace in you. Help me not to put more emphasis on situations but more emphasis on finding peace in every situation. Thank you for your love and for being the Prince of Peace. Amen!

53

HOT TEA

"And the God of all grace, who called you to his eternal glory in Christ, after you have suffered a little while, will himself restore you and make you strong, firm and steadfast." —I Peter 5:10

I absolutely love hot tea. Hot tea soothes my throat and helps me to relax. At home, I have all sorts and varieties of teas from everywhere. My very favorite store to purchase tea from is my neighborhood HEB. My favorite place to get a hot tea beverage to drink on the way to work or home is Starbucks. What I love about tea is that it takes hot water to bring out the hot flavor of any tea. Putting tea in cold water will not have the same effect as hot water. You see, we all are tea bags, and in order to get the best out of us, God allows the hot water to cultivate us into the man and woman that we will become. With adversity on the job, God is brewing you for greatness. With disappointment from a family member or friend, God is teaching you to have patience. The more challenging the situation, the more God is preparing you for a greater blessing.

I Peter 5:10 reads, "And the God of all grace, who called you to his eternal glory in Christ, after you have suffered a little while, will himself restore you and make you strong, firm and steadfast." Think about the tea bag in the hot water; the longer it sits in the hot water, the better it tastes. To make the tea taste better, sometimes you add lemons, peppermint, and a drop of honey. As we are being brewed to greatness, God the Father is with us every step of the way, which represents the squeezing of the lemon. The peppermint resembles Jesus because He intercedes for you. The Honey is the Holy Spirit who comforts you and guides your path. It is good to know that you may resemble a tea bag, but God renews you every day to bring forth the best fruits and the best character and to make you a great believer. Thank God for the hot water, which represents the challenges that make you stronger and better. James 2: 2-4 reads, "Consider it pure joy, my brothers and sisters, whenever you face trials of many kinds, because you know that the testing of your faith produces perseverance. Let perseverance finish its work so that you may be mature and complete, not lacking anything." More importantly, it is a blessing to be a vessel for the Lord. Amen!!!

THINK IT OVER POINTS:

1. How has adversity made you stronger or better in your life?
2. Name a time in your life when you felt stuck and it took a challenge to move forward.

Prayer: Lord, we thank you for hot tea because just like tea tastes better in hot water, so do we get better after enduring trials and tribulations. I thank you for being with me as I endure difficulty and because you are my Heavenly Father, and I am never alone. Thank you for allowing me to see the beauty and blessings of adversity. Amen.

54

REBIRTH

"He saved us, not because of righteous things we had done, but because of his mercy. He saved us through the washing of rebirth and renewal by the Holy Spirit." **—Titus 3:5**

As you are reborn in Christ, you are on a whole new level of blessings. Your life changes, and even your thought processes are different. Why are they different? God is in your life, and you need to seek him before making frivolous decisions. You can now sit at the welcome table of the Father, the Son, and the Holy Spirit. The angels in heaven are rejoicing and celebrating with you. You just gave the devil a black eye.

As you learn and grow, it is your responsibility to bring others to Christ. You are now a living vessel to bring more soldiers into the body of Christ. Bring joy to our Heavenly Father by telling others about the goodness of God. Amen.

THINK IT OVER POINTS:

1. Why is rebirth important in your life?
2. How many people have you witnessed about Jesus Christ?

Prayer: God, thank you for the new and rebirth in me. Lord, help me focus on doing your will and walking circumspectly to your word. Lord, help me love others and win them over to Christ. Amen!

55

YOUR ASSIGNMENT

"Therefore do not be foolish, but understand what the Lord's will is." —Ephesians 5:17

I love going shoe shopping because I get to try boots, heels, and sneakers and I just adore how my feet look in the mirror. I wear a 9 and sometimes 9.5, but it really depends on the shoe. Needless to say, sandals are what I live for, especially after having a pedicure. Once, I tried on a shoe that was an 8.5, and right away, I knew it was not a good fit. Just like the 8.5 was not the right fit, so is doing an assignment that God has not called you to do. You are out of place and out of order when you are out of the will of God. Ephesians 5:17 reads, "Therefore do not be foolish, but understand what the Lord's will is."

Stop giving yourself assignments that did not come from God. We have volunteered for things that God has not called us to do, and then when we become stuck, we want the Lord to bail us out. I am guilty as charged because I have been on all types of committees in church, at work, and in social organizations. One committee that I was on was not assigned by God; I was miserable. I mean Miserable with a capital M. I let people talk me onto the ledge, which caused me to jump into activities or committees that were not a perfect fit for me. But I prayed to God, "Lord, it's me, and I am for real. If you get me out of this, I will not self-assign myself to things you didn't give me permission to participate. I once went into a business, which I knew darn well that that was not the assignment from God. I lost money, time, and friendship. My spiritual gift is not being a salesman, but I do have the gift of shopping. Stick with the assignments given to you by God and not by man. My family and friends who truly know me understand that I do not help people move anywhere. That is not my gift. I will visit you after you unpack, and then I will come over. I am so serious, and I am being for real. We must line up with the will of God. Proverbs 19:21 reads, "Many are the plans in a person's heart, but it is the Lord's purpose that prevails." If we do what the Lord expects, we will be richly blessed. I think before I speak. I immediately say no if it has not been designated by God. I stay in a size 9, and I don't try to wear a size 8.5. I stay at the address assigned to me, and I do not try to relocate to a new or different assignment where I might live in misery. Stay at the assignment, see it through, and trust in God. Amen!

THINK IT OVER POINTS:

1. How do you know when you are not doing God's assignment?
2. What can prevent you from doing God's assignment?

Prayer: Lord, thank you for the assignment you gave me. Thank you for reminding me why I was assigned to the assignment in the first place. Father God, help me to do your will instead of doing the will of others' self-assignments. Amen!!

56

IT'S OK TO SAY NO

---

*"For I know the plans I have for you, declares the Lord, plans to prosper you and not to harm you, plans to give you hope and a future." — **Jeremiah 29:11***

---

have a friend who will do anything and everything for everybody. She has the gift of not being able to say no. Guess what, my friend? People take advantage of her, and God does not want us to be abused. Jeremiah 29:11 says, "For I know the plans I have for you, declares the Lord, plans to prosper you and not to harm you, plans to give you hope and a future." There is nothing wrong with saying no to something you cannot do. People will treat you the way you allow them to treat you, whether good or bad. As people of God, we must know our worth. Psalms 139:14 says, "I will praise thee; for I am fearfully and wonderfully made: marvellous are thy works; and that my soul knoweth right well". God made you for a purpose not to be used and abused by others.

Luke 12:6-7 illustrates just how much we are worth. It reads: "Are not five sparrows sold for two pennies? Yet not one of them is forgotten by God. Indeed, the very hairs of your head are all numbered. Don't be afraid; you are worth more than many sparrows." God loves you and values you, so know that you are worth much more to God than anything. If God loves you, you must also love and appreciate yourself. No is a Strong and Powerful word. Try it today and see how much better you feel and how less stressed out you will become—sigh of relief. I just entered the room to save you. Let the church say, Amen. Amen!

THINK IT OVER POINTS:

1. Why is it so hard to say no to family and friends?
2. Do you think people are afraid to tell you no?

Prayer: Heavenly Father, thank you for blessing me to say "no." Saying no to people will not stop me from receiving my blessings from you. My main purpose in life is to please you, and less concerned about pleasing man. Thank you for the blessing to know that I can rest in you to know I made the right choice and not being pressured to do something that my heart was not in it. Amen.

57

I AM BETTER THAN THAT

"So we fix our eyes not on what is seen, but on what is unseen, since what is seen is temporary, but what is unseen is eternal. " **—2 Corinthians 4:18**

---

have been blessed. I am great. I am thankful. I am who God created me to be, So I will stop thinking of myself in a negative manner. I will disregard comments that will tear me down. I will only engage in conversation with people who build me up, and that will not tear me down. I found favor with the Lord, so I am better than that. I am better than what the world said that I was. I may not have accomplished all things in my life, but I am grateful to have accomplished most things. I am set apart from everyone else. I am God's special design. There is no other person made like me or designed like the way my Heavenly Father made me.

2 Corinthians 4:18 reads, "So we fix our eyes not on what is seen, but on what is unseen, since what is seen is

temporary, but what is unseen is eternal." Criticism of love is accepted. Belittling me will be rejected. Compliments in love are accepted. Negative remarks about me are rejected. I am better than all the nay-sayers, the haters, my enemies, and so-called friends. I walk closer with my friends and even closer with my enemies. I am very ready to test the road of my faith and the promises of God. I can outstand and outlast anyone who tries to bring me foolery. I am God's child and God's servant. I am anointed, and if you mess with me, know that I don't have to say a word because God covers my front and my back. I am better than who I was... I am a servant in God's army. Amen!

THINK IT OVER POINTS:

1. How can I stay focused on things that are of God?
2. How do you know that you are set apart from everything else?

Prayer: Thank you for keeping me whole when man tries to break me into pieces, but I am better than that. Keep me humble so that the love of God will always shine inside out. Bless me to always give you thanks for all the many blessings that you give me daily. Amen.

58

MERCY SHOWS UP

"Because of the LORD's great love we are not consumed, for his compassions never fail. They are new every morning; great is your faithfulness.."
—Lamentations 3:22-23

I have a son and daughter, and they are very close, but every now and then, they may have a disagreement. Most siblings will fight or argue about various matters. And when they have a disagreement, I really want to intervene, but sometimes I can't. I try to talk to both of them separately because when they are angry, they do not want to talk. Mercy, Lord, is all I can say. My grandmother always said, "Lord, have mercy on me. It may take weeks for my children to get back together, but when mercy shows up, things begin to change. God gives us grace and mercy every day, not just any mercy, but new mercies. Lamentations 3:23 reads, "Through the Lord's mercies we are not consumed, Because His compassions fail not." God shows mercy for us, but we are not quick to show mercy for others.

When my children were younger, I could make them do what I needed them to do with some coercion, but when they became young adults, that authority was gone. My authority over them may be gone, but not the authority of my Heavenly Father. Hebrews 4:16 says, "Let us then approach God's throne of grace with confidence, so that we may receive mercy and find grace to help us in our time of need. When mercy shows up, it changes the atmosphere in all situations. Mercy is just the compassion of love that God shows His people when he does not have to. The best part of it all is Micah 7:18, which reads, "Who is a God like you, who pardons sin and forgives the transgression of the remnant of his inheritance? You do not stay angry forever but be delighted to show mercy." God desires and wants to give you mercy so that you can show mercy to others. Have you shown mercy to someone today? If not, then work on making it happen. Amen!

Think it over points:

1. Why is it important to show mercy to others?
2. Does God often show mercy to you even when you don't deserve it?

Prayer: Heavenly Father, thank you for blessing me to show mercy to others. Let us cover each other's faults instead of bringing judgment. Lord, we know when mercy shows up, grace and love are at the door of our hearts. Amen.

59

RISE UP

"Let us not become weary in doing good, for at the proper time we will reap a harvest if we do not give up." —Galatians 6:9

You may go down, but don't stay down—men and women of God, you need to rise up. I have encountered many students, and some were very smart, but others needed a lot of support. Jeremy struggled in Math and Reading and almost gave up on school and life. He had been told he was dumb, he was worthless, and would not turn out to be anything great. Galatians 6:9 says, "Let us not become weary in doing good, for at the proper time we will reap a harvest if we do not give up." He almost gave up, but I encouraged him to rise out of that situation. He worked hard and did not quit, and God blessed him to pass his state test. He had felt that his goals were unreachable, but he started seeing the light. No matter how Jeremy wanted to quit, I pushed him to stay on course. James 4:8 reads, "Come near to God and he will come near to you. Wash your hands, you sinners, and purify your hearts, you double-minded."

If you stay your course near the Lord, no obstacle will deter you from reaching your blessings. Amen.

THINK IT OVER POINTS:

1. Why do you think it is easy for people to quit?
2. What are some ways that you can encourage yourself when you feel that you are alone?

Prayer: Father God, thank you for enabling me to Rise Up. Thank you for helping me to see that even when life gives me a bad hand, I can rise up in every situation. Also, continue to bless me to see the good in everything and everyone. I will not complain if I have misfortunes because I have the greatest blessing in my life, which is you as my Heavenly Father.

60

HOMERUN

"Whatever you do, work heartily, as for the Lord and not for men." — Colossians 3:23

My husband and family are Houston Astros fans. They love the Astros, and when someone hits a home run while the bases are loaded, the crowd goes wild, and my family is right along with them. As Christians, we should be hitting home runs in our walk for Jesus. We need to be about the work of Jesus Christ. We must put in the time to get to know Him more and get to know His people. Our life should resemble His life. Colossians 3:23 says, "Whatever you do, work heartily, as for the Lord and not for men."

A great way to win people over to Christ is to be an example by treating people kindly, even when people are unkind to you. I know what you are about to say, "If a person is unkind to me, then I will return the favor." That is not the work of the Lord. I would not want to miss heaven by being unkind to others. Colossians 3:17 reads, "And whatever you do, in word or deed, do everything in the name of the Lord Jesus, giving thanks to God the Father through him. Just like the hitter makes sure the ball goes out of the park for the homerun, we too, should be making important connections with God's people. We need to hit home runs every day as we build relationships with God's people and with each other. Amen!

THINK IT OVER POINTS:

1. Why is it important to make connection with God's people?
2. Does building a relationship with God's people help to stay connected to God?

Prayer: Heavenly Father, thank you for the home runs in our lives. Being able to be an example for others to see is a blessing for you. As we get up to start a whole new baseball game of life, let us make positive impressions on others so they, too, will get to know you. Amen!

61

FIGURE IT OUT

*"But may the righteous be glad and rejoice before God; may they be happy and joyful." —**Psalm 68: 3***

Sometimes, I have a tendency to overbook my schedule. Between work, family, and my own self-care life, it can become overwhelming. Things are not always going to work out, but with determination and enduring power, they eventually will. However, you must figure it out. You must figure out what brings you sadness and what brings you joy. Psalm 68: 3 reads, "But may the righteous be glad and rejoice before God; may they be happy and joyful.." If people around you bring you sadness, you need to figure out how to make new friends with people who are like-minded. Philippians 2:5 reads, "Let this mind be in you, which was also in Christ Jesus." Suppose all that you have around you is negativity. In that case, you need to be able to have a positive presence that enables you to celebrate the goodness of God. 1

Thessalonians 5: 16-18 states, "Rejoice evermore. Pray without ceasing. In everything give thanks: for this is the will of God in Christ Jesus concerning you."

God wants you to be happy, healthy, and whole, and sometimes, the people around you bring you the most sadness and heartache. Figure out what brings you the most happiness and gravitate towards those things. Psalm 16:11 reads, "Thou wilt shew me the path of life: in thy presence *is* fulness of joy; at thy right hand *there are* pleasures for evermore." Figure it out through prayer and supplication. Philippians 4:6 states, "Be careful about nothing, but in everything by prayer and supplication with thanksgiving let your requests be made known unto God." Make sure you figure it out by seeking the kingdom of God first. Matthew 6:33 reads, "But seek first the kingdom of God and His righteousness, and all these things shall be added to you." Figure it out by doing what is holy and acceptable. Romans 12:1 states, " I beseech you therefore, brethren, by the mercies of God, that ye present your bodies a living sacrifice, holy, acceptable unto God, which is your reasonable service." All of the questions can be figured out by talking to God and being humble in God's presence.

THINK IT OVER POINTS:

1. Why do you think that when you figure things out early, things turn out differently?
2. What are some warning signs that you know a person is not for you?

Prayer: Father, thank you for blessing me to find my way by figuring it out through you. Let me always be open to your will and to your way. Let me always keep you first in every aspect of my life. Amen!

62

WIGGLE ROOM

"When a man's ways please the Lord, he maketh even his enemies to be at peace with him. Better is a little with righteousness than great revenues without right. A man's heart deviseth his way: but the Lord directeth his steps. A divine sentence is in the lips of the king: his mouth transgresseth not in judgment." —Proverbs 16: 7-10

Have you ever been stuck after trying to look for something that was in a hole or underneath a surface? Maybe your drainage pipe had a major clog, and you had to get a plumber. Life sometimes will have you stuck in a place where you cannot get out. Proverbs 16: 7-10 says, "When a man's ways please the Lord, he maketh even his enemies to be at peace with him. Better is a little with righteousness than great revenues without right. A man's heart deviseth his way: but the Lord directeth his steps. A divine sentence is in the lips of the king: his mouth transgresseth not in judgment." God gives us just enough wiggle room to get out of tight situations.

God always has a ram in the bush. Numbers 6:24-26 reads, "The Lord bless you and keep you; the Lord make his face shine on you and be gracious to you; the Lord turn his face toward you and give you peace.'" That is the wiggle room. You feel like your life is about to collapse, but God always gives you wiggle room so that you can see He is with you. When you feel as though you are going in circles, God has a way of slowing down the day so you can think about His goodness and mercy, which keep you all day and all night. When you have been denied a promotion, but God gives you a bigger promotion, and you are now over the boss who was giving you a hard time. That is a wiggle room blessing. God allows you to push ahead just enough so that you know He has never left. Wiggle room is that comfort God provides when you feel like you are all alone, but you are not alone because He is right there by your side. Amen.

THINK IT OVER POINTS:

1. Can you think of the wiggle room God has done for you this morning? How about yesterday?
2. Think and ask yourself this: is God's timing the right timing?

Prayer: God, thank you for wiggle room blessings. Lord, thank you for giving me comfort with wiggle room when things seem like they are out of control and for allowing me to still find peace in a time of a storm. Lord, thank you for the Wiggle room that enables me to take deep breaths when I cannot go any further, and God blesses me without a second thought. Amen!

63

RAMEN NOODLES ARE NOT THAT BAD

"I will praise You, O Lord, with my whole heart; I will tell of all Your marvelous works." —Psalm 9:1

College students are some poor individuals. I remember being in the dorm room and having to leave to get food from the cafeteria. I did not enjoy eating the food on campus because the cafeteria food was not good at all. It was not seasoned, and it was not a home-cooked meal, but when I made it back to my room, I had a plan. If a plan was not in place, you would be hungry, so Ramen noodles are not that bad. I did not know how blessed I was, but there is always someone in a worse situation than you.

Psalm 9:1 reads, "I will praise *You,* O Lord, with my whole heart; I will tell of all Your marvelous works." I do not know if you know this, but God is marvelous. You are blessed if you have food to eat because somebody somewhere is hungry. You are blessed that God allowed you another opportunity to wake up this morning. Psalm 35:18 reads, "I will give thee thanks in the great congregation: I will praise thee among many people." Being able to thank God for Ramen noodles is a blessing. Some people may not think Ramon noodles are not much, but they may be more than what others have. Psalm 69:30 reads, "I will praise the name of God with a song, and will magnify him with thanksgiving." I have thankfulness in my spirit for God being God all by himself. Ramen noodles are not that bad because they are a reminder of just how much God has blessed me. I will forever thank the Lord. Thank you. Amen.

THINK IT OVER POINTS:

1. Have you thought just how blessed you are?
2. Have you thought that you did not have much until you talked to a friend?

Prayer: Heavenly Father, thank you for the humble beginnings. I am grateful for Ramen noodles because they are not that bad. Lord, enable me to appreciate the many blessings and to continue counting my blessings. There is always someone else who wishes to be in my shoes. Amen!

64

LIVE WITH THE DECISION YOU MAKE

"When a man's ways please the Lord, he maketh even his enemies to be at peace with him."
—Proverbs 16:7

t is amazing growing up with teenagers. They do some funny stuff, and they do things that we said they should not do, but they must live with the decisions that they make. Those are teenagers. What about you, a Bible-Filled Bible Scholar? God has put detour signs all around the construction site, but you don't yield. You take routes moving full speed ahead. Proverbs 16:7 reads, "When a man's ways please the Lord, he maketh even his enemies to be at peace with him." When you intentionally and purposely walk in the will of God, you have no regrets because God is leading you.

When you find yourself making decisions that God did not give you permission for, you must live with the consequences of the decisions you make. All decisions which are not God-led have a consequence. Some of the consequences you make may be life-changing, and others may lead to a tragedy where you cannot recover. If you let God guide you, things will be much better in your life. Psalm 37: 3-4 tells us to, "Trust in the Lord, and do good; so shalt thou dwell in the land, and verily thou shalt be fed. Delight thyself also in the Lord: and he shall give thee the desires of thine heart." Isaiah 48:17 says, "Thus saith the Lord, thy Redeemer, the Holy One of Israel; I am the Lord thy God which teacheth thee to profit, which leadeth thee by the way that thou shouldest go." Walking with God is safe proof because it prevents you from living with the decisions you should not have made.

Think It Over Points:

1. Are you living with some decisions that you have made that are irreversible?
2. Can you think of some situations in which you yielded to God, and it turned out to be the best decision ever?

Prayer: Father God, help me walk closer to you. If I falter, Lord, let me learn from my mistake and move on. Enable me not to stay down in the pit, but help me to come out of it with thanksgiving and praise in my heart. Amen!

65

ARE YOU PERFECT IN CHRIST?

" For it is by grace you have been saved, through faith—and this is not from ourselves, it is the gift of God— not by works, so that no one can boast. "
—Ephesians 2:8-9

I believe that we are very hard on other people, but we are not hard on ourselves. We judge people, and we have not taken the time to look in the mirror to see our own flaws. Ephesians 2:8-9 reads, "For it is by grace you have been saved, through faith—and this is not from ourselves, it is the gift of God— not by works, so that no one can boast." God's amazing grace kept us and saved us. It is through grace and grace alone that we are saved. I cannot see your flaws because I am too busy being fixated on my own flaws. Each and every day, I am trying to see what needs to be changed in my life so that I can please God. My life is not my own because it belongs to God. I do not bother about things that are not of God.

I once had a person come to me and complained about everything. Then, it became a constant complaint about someone else every day. He does not do this, and he does not do that. I quietly told the individual there are many people that do not do their job. We cannot complain about them unless we complain about everyone. Romans 3:23 reads, "For all have sinned and fall short of the glory of God." There is not a person on earth that is perfect except Jesus Christ. The point I attempted to make is that there is no perfect person on our jobs, but we can model the expectations for the job. I do not do everything right at my job, at home, with my spouse, with my children, with my family, and at church, but I sure work on ways that I can correct behavior that God does not approve of.

I look in the mirror daily and ask, "God, did I handle this correctly, and was I polite?" There are going to be days when you get it right and other days when you get it wrong, but you must keep working at it every day. Philippians 3:14 reads, "I press toward the mark for the prize of the high calling of God in Christ Jesus." My daily walk is to please God, make peace with people, show love to mankind, and do the will of my Heavenly Father. I will never be perfect, but my daily aim is to line up with the perfect will of God. Amen.

THINK IT OVER POINTS:

1. Do you have flaws that can be improved?
2. Name something that can be changed in your life that will make you more attractive to doing God's will.

Prayer: Heavenly Father, help me to be more like you. Enable me to look into the mirror each and every day so that I can resemble you. Let me move more rapidly when I have not done your will, and help me correct the errors in my ways. Amen!!

66

ROADBLOCKS AND DETOURS

"For I, the LORD your God, hold your right hand; it is I who say to you, "Fear not, I am the one who helps you." —Isaiah 41:13

I live in a large city and traffic is bad, so there are many freeways but still much traffic. If you pay for the tollway, then you may be in less traffic just a bit. I travel on the Grandparkway quite a bit. It is faster and less traffic. Sometimes, when I am driving around the city, there will be roadblocks and detours. It can be frustrating if I have to take a different route. Besides delays and being upset about unforeseen circumstances, you must be able to roll with the flow. Once you get through traffic, you make it to your destination. There is no reason in the world to fret or be upset anymore. No matter what is going on, God will help you. Isaiah 41:13 reads, "For I, the LORD your God, hold your right hand; it is I who say to you, "Fear not, I am the one who helps you."

Life has roadblocks and detours, and it is how you handle them that determines your success. Complaining and whining do not change anything about the mishap. You are just making noise. Why not celebrate that you are an overcomer with God? 1 John 4:4 reads, "Little children, you are from God and have overcome them, for he who is in you is greater than he who is in the world." We must thank God for all his many blessings.

1 Corinthians 15:57 reads, "But thanks be to God, who gives us the victory through our Lord Jesus Christ." If you have a roadblock in life, find a way around the problem. 1 John 5:4-5 reads, "For everyone who has been born of God overcomes the world. And this is the victory that has overcome the world—our faith. Who is it that overcomes the world except for the one who believes that Jesus is the Son of God?" Even if you have a detour in your life or a sudden unexpected change, is God not with you? Yes, God is with each and every one of us, so we must be able to go through it without frowning but with a smile. Joshua 1: 9 reads, "Have I not commanded you? Be strong and courageous. Do not be afraid; do not be discouraged, for the Lord your God will be with you wherever you go." Roadblocks and detours are made for you to trust through every path and every obstacle. Amen!

THINK IT OVER POINTS:

1. What are the benefits of roadblocks and detours?
2. How have life adjustments made you stronger and wiser?

Prayer: God, thank you for roadblocks and detours. I have been blessed beyond measure because of your goodness and mercy. No matter what is going on in my life, you will never leave me or forsake me. Amen!!

67

GOLF MOVES

---

*"That ye may be the children of your Father which is in heaven: for he maketh his sun to rise on the evil and on the good, and sendeth rain on the just and on the unjust." — **Matthews 5:45***

I know so many people that enjoy the world of golf. My husband and father-in-law get joy out of going golfing. I asked my husband why he loves it, and he said, "It relaxes my mind, and you can simply take your time to do it. It is as if you don't have a care in the world." I started thinking because it should be that way when we are on a daily walk with God. We are going to take a swing at life, and some days it is going to be a hit, and other days it will be a miss, but God is at every place in life, which is our golf course. Matthews 5:45 reads, "That ye may be the children of your Father which is in heaven: for he maketh his sun to rise on the evil and on the good, and sendeth rain on the just and on the unjust." In golf moves, if you fail, you get to start over on the next game with a fresh start. No one throws in your face that you are a failure. You either have a good golf game or a bad one, but it is the game you play, and every day, you are not going to be a winner.

Somedays in life, you are going to get a hole-in-one, which means everything went well at work, with the kids, the spouse is great, and it is just a perfect kind of day. Lamentations 3:22-23 reads, "It is of the Lord's mercies that we are not consumed, because his compassions fail not. They are new every morning: great is thy faithfulness." Every day will not be that way, but you must still keep going and stay focused on God's word, how He has blessed you, how He has sustained, and how He has been your everything. 1 Peter 5:7 reads, "Casting all your care upon him; for he careth for you." In golf moves, there is no rush to finish the game. There is patience even if you miss a shot and have to wait for your next turn, you simply relax and enjoy the presence of God. It is kind of like your whole world may be upside down, but you are not even bothered because God has control of the game. The benefit of golf moves is that God determines the ending of the last stroke when you relax in Him and just breathe and listen to the voice of God.

Think it over points:

1. How important is it to listen to the voice of God and wait on God's timing?
2. What can be learned in a day, whether it is a hit or a miss?

Prayer: God, thank you for the golf moves. Enable me to take my time in life and not try to get in a hurry to do anything. I know that life can be a hit or miss, but it enables us to see the best and the good in every situation. Amen.

68

APPRECIATE PEOPLE IN YOUR LIFE

"Be kind and compassionate to one another, forgiving each other, just as in Christ God forgave you." —Ephesians 4:32

Life is short, and it is not every day that good people come into your life. Every day should be a day of thanksgiving for the people that are important to you. Ephesians 4:32 reads, "Be kind and compassionate to one another, forgiving each other, just as in Christ God forgave you." If you are fortunate to have a spouse, thank God for him. Thank God for the things that he does for you. 1 John 4:16 reads, "And so we know and rely on the love God has for us. God is love. Whoever lives in love lives in God, and God in them." Appreciate the smile, kindness, and love that he shows you daily. If you have children, tell them every day that you love them. Each and every day, give them praise, words of encouragement, and a smile. Let them know they are valuable and important to you. If you have family and friends who adore you and appreciate you, let them know that they are important as well.

John 15:12-13 reads, "My command is this: Love each other as I have loved you. Greater love has no one than this: to lay down one's life for one's friends." Support them the way they support you. Find ways to encourage them when they feel down and out. Galatians 6:2 reads, "Carry each other's burdens, and in this way you will fulfill the law of Christ." Lift up their spirits when they feel that they cannot go on. Proverbs 17:17 reads, "A friend loves at all times, and a brother is born for a time of adversity." Build them up when they are torn down. Let them know that you are in their corner. Tomorrow is not promised, so you must live today as if it is the only time left. Make sure you love one another and show forgiveness and grace to others. Let God's love shine through and through. Amen!!

THINK IT OVER POINTS:

1. Do you only show love and grace to the people that you know?
2. What adjustments can you make to show the people that you love and that you care about them?

Prayer: Dear Heavenly Father, thank you for putting people in my life that love me. You have placed people in my life for a reason, and since they are there, I must show them that I care just as much about them as they care for me. Let me wake up each morning and show love to them and all of your people. Amen.

69

YOUR DADDY KNOWS

"Trust in the Lord with all your heart and lean not on your own understanding; in all your ways submit to him, and he will make your paths straight."
—Proverbs 3:5-6

There is nothing that God does not know about His children. Your Daddy knows about your highs and your lows. He knows when you are hurt and just need to lay in His arms, but even when things are going wrong, He still wants you to trust Him. Sometimes, we just have to trust the process when we do not know what to do. Proverbs 3:5-6 reads, "Trust in the Lord with all your heart and lean not on your own understanding; in all your ways submit to him, and he will make your paths straight."

When I was in the sixth grade, the reading teacher had a contest, and I was super excited to participate. The winner would win a surprise if he/she did what was required. I won, but I did not want to receive the prize.

My Heavenly Father knew I felt hurt and rejected, and He gave me comfort during my sadness. Again, your Daddy knows, but you must remember to go to God in prayer. James 5:13 reads, "Is anyone among you in trouble? Let them pray. Is anyone happy? Let them sing songs of praise." Your Daddy knows and will give comfort in the time of need. Romans 8:26 states, "In the same way, the Spirit helps us in our weakness. We do not know what we ought to pray for, but the Spirit himself intercedes for us through wordless groans."

Some things will happen in your life that come out of nowhere, but I have learned to breathe, rest in God, pray, and leave it with my Daddy. Your Daddy knows and will definitely guide you in the direction you need to go in. Amen!

THINK IT OVER POINTS:

1. Can you name a time that you thought God did not know that experiencing trouble or heartache?
2. Difficult times are periods when you should trust in God the most. If that is the case, then why don't you trust Him in those times?

Prayer: Heavenly Father, thank you for always knowing what goes on in my life. Help me to trust you and the process when my life may be going haywire. Help me to pray, chew on your word, take deep breaths, and know that you are going to work everything out for my good. Amen!

70

SILENCE IS GOLDEN

"In the morning, Lord, you hear my voice; in the morning I lay my requests before you and wait expectantly." **—Psalm 5:3**

One faithful day, I had to catch a ride to work with my BFF because I would need to pick up a car later on from the rental place. As she was driving, she said, "Girl, I must let you know that I ride in silence." I said, "Oh, ok." It never hit me what that meant until this morning when I was riding to work. The radio was off, and I was in harmony with the peace and presence of God being with me as I rode to work. Psalm 5:3 reads, "In the morning, Lord, you hear my voice; in the morning, I lay my requests before you and wait expectantly."

Being able to ride in silence and only hear the voice of God was a blessing. When alone with God, you tune out all the unwanted distractions. Psalm 85:8 reads, "I will hear what God the Lord will speak, For He will speak peace to

His people and to His saints; But let them not turn back to folly." It is a great and wonderful time to meditate on God's goodness and blessings. You are not thinking about work, family, problems, or anything else, but you are just in the moment of awe and the amazement of how good God is in every aspect of your life. Amen!

THINK IT OVER POINTS:

1. How can silence enable you to be more attuned to God?
2. Name ways of how quiet and silence is a great way to focus on God's love for you.

Prayer: Thank you, Lord, for allowing me to hear your voice when I am alone and without any distractions. I am thankful that I am blessed to be in your presence any time of the day. I appreciate you blessing me and giving me guidance and comfort daily. Amen.